Library of Congress Catalog Card Number:
ISBN: 2009936238
        0-9759601-8-0

Prepare Yourself and Speak

Ahmad H. Sakr, Ph.D.

Published by:
Foundation for Islamic Knowledge
P.O. Box 665
Lombard, Illinois 60148 (USA)
Telephone: (630) 495-4817
FAX: (630) 627-8894
Tax I.D #36-377-4566
E-mail: drhmadsakr@hotmail.com
Website: www.ahmadsakr.com

God's Majesty Exalted

This book is dedicated to Allah Ta'ala (Almighty) for all the favors He has bestowed upon me in creating and bringing me to this world. His Love, His Mercy, His Compassion, His Forgiveness, His Graciousness, His Kindness and His Bountifulness are above any humble person like me, to be able to thank Him enough and to praise Him.

O Allah!   I am humbly dedicating this work **to You.**

O Allah!   Accept my humble work and help me disseminate the information to those who need it.

O Allah!   Make this humble work worthy **of You.**

O Allah!   Forgive my shortcomings.

O Allah!   Help me live as a Muslim and die as a Mu'min (Believer).

O Allah!   Let me be summoned on the Day of Judgment with Prophet Muhammad (pbuh), with the other Prophets, the martyrs and all the noble believers. Ameen.

Table of Contents

Prepare Yourself and Speak

Title   **Page No.**

Title   **Page No.**

In the name of Allah, the Most
Merciful, The Ever Lasting Mercy.

Acknowledgements   كلمة شكر

•   The author wishes to thank all those friends who helped him in making this book and the previous books available to the readers. Special thanks go to Dr. Yusuf Kamaluddin (Yao-Keng) Chang and his wife, Audrey, for their tremendous help and moral support during the last few years. Thanks and appreciations go to the Vakil families (Abu Bakr, Usman, Farouq, Ishaq, Iqbal, and Akhtar) for their support to the author and the Foundation. May Allah (swt) bless them and bless their late parents (Umar and Amina). Thanks and appreciations go to Dr. and Mrs. Ahmed K. Noor for taking care of the Newsletter: **Perspectives** for a number of years and from their own personal expenses.

•   Moreover, the author wishes to thank all the respected brothers and sisters who have helped previously and are still helping. Among the many are Mr. Asad Khan and his wife, Sister Azma Khan; Dr. and Mrs. Mohammed Shafi; Mr. & Mrs. Javed Habib; Mr. & Mrs. Abdul Wahab; Mr. & Mrs. Saghir Aslam; Dr. & Mrs. Nadim Daouk; Mr. Refat M. Abo Elela; Dr. & Mrs. Zeyd A. Merenkov; Dr. and Mrs. Daudur Rahman; Mr. and Mrs. Shakeel Syed; Dr. and Mrs. Maqbool Ahmad; Mr. Zia Khan and his wife Tina Khan; Dr. and Mrs. Syed A. Zahir; Dr. and Mrs. Muhammad K. Zaman; Dr. and Mrs. Mostapha Arafa; Dr. & Mrs. Samir Arafeh; Dr. M. Munir Chaudry and his family; the late Dr. F.R. Khan and his respected wife Sister Farhat Khan, may Allah (swt) bless his soul, and many more.

•   Thanks and appreciation goes to Dr. Dany Doueiri for translating some chapters from Arabic to English, as well as typing the Arabic texts and index of some books. May Allah bless him and reward him and his family. Ameen. Special thanks and appreciations go to Sister Fawzia Akalal; Sister Sajeda Sultani and her family; Sister Houyda Najjar Mertaban and her family; Brother Mohammed Bilal Khan and his family; and Brother Waseem Najmi and his wife Yasmeen for their kind help in many areas.

vi

- Also our thanks and appreciation is extended to Sister Azizah Abdul Rahman of Singapore, on behalf of her late parents Aminah Bint Ahmad and Abdul Rahman bin Mohamed. May Allah (swt) be pleased with her and her late parents. Ameen.

- Special thanks and appreciations go to Sister Shadia Hassan and her children for their help, advice, and contributions for the love of Allah (swt). Our prayers of Maghfirah for her late husband Mr. Samir Hassan and her late father Mr. Ahmad Ali. May Allah (swt) bless their souls and make their final stay in Paradise. Ameen. We are thankful and grateful to Mr. Muhammad El-Bdeiwi and his family for their generosity in helping this Foundation for Da'wah purposes. Our thanks also go to Mr. & Mrs. Abu Ramy Assaf, as well as to Dr. Yusuf K. Deshmukh and his family. Our thanks and appreciations go to Mr. Ammar Charani and his brother Samer Charani of Muslim Education Funds (MEF) for their help. May Allah (swt) bless them all. Our thanks go to Mr. Anwar Haq and his wife Blanca Haq and family members for their moral support to this Foundation.

- Thanks and appreciations go to Mr. Khaled Obagi for his support to the Foundation on behalf of his late father and mother Aref Obagi and Nabila Al-Beik. Our thanks and appreciations also go to Mr. Ahmad Al-Khatib for his support to the Foundation on behalf of his mother Soraya, and his late father Adel Baheej Al-Khatib. Thanks and appreciation also goes to Dr. Osama Haikal on behalf of his late father, Mr. Omar Haikal. May Allah (swt) be pleased with them and may Allah (swt) keep their relatives in Paradise. Ameen. Our thanks and affections go to Brother Fathy Haggag and his family for their tremendous support to the author for all the years in California. It is only Allah (swt) Who will reward them. Our heartfelt thank to my brother, Samir and his family for their excellent management of this Foundation.

- Thanks and appreciations go to Sister Sadia Rahman and her late mother Javaid Akhtar Rahman for her support to this Foundation. Thanks and appreciations to Abu Firas and Umm Firas Meher as well as Br. Ali Al-Najjar for their support of the Masjid (IEC) and Da'wah through literature.

- Thanks and appreciations go also to Dr. Muhammad Waleed Khalife and his family for their support to this Foundation. Moreover, our thanks and appreciation go to Dr. Syed A. Rizvi and his family for their personal help to the author and to this Foundation. May Allah bless them and reward them. Ameen.

- Thanks and appreciations are to Mr. Kamel Daouk and his brothers who helped this Foundation by supplying papers for printing the books. Yes Indeed! We are thankful and grateful to Brother Hassan Igram who is the president of Cedar Graphics Company, and who has been helping this Foundation for the last 35 years by printing most of the books. Moreover, we are thankful to Mr. Anwer Khan and his brothers of A-1 Printing and Graphics who helped this Foundation by printing a good number of pamphlets. May Allah (swt) bless all of them. Ameen. We are thankful to Brother Talal Smadi who contributed the Arabic typesetting for this Book and previous ones.

- Last but not least, my thanks, appreciation and love are to my wife, Zuhar Barhumi Sakr and our loving children: Sara and her husband Mohamad Nasser and their children Nada, Abdul Rahman, Ibrahim, Jenna, Hannah, Amber, Sabrina and youngest son Adam; to Hussein and his wife Dania and daughters Ayah, Dana and Noor; to Jihad and his wife Nasrin, son Hamza and the twins daughters Sumayyah and Sawsan; to Basil and his wife La Reina and daughters Amina, Randa, Yasmine and son Jibreel. *We pray to Allah (swt) to open the hearts of other friends to invest with Allah (swt).*

- The author prays to Allah (swt) to bless Prophet Muhammad and the family of Prophet Muhammad (pbuh), in as much as He blessed Prophet Ibrahim and the family of Prophet Ibrahim (pbuh). The author also prays to Allah (swt) to bless the Khulafaa' Rashidoon (Rightly guided) and the Sahaba (Companions) of the Prophet (pbuh) as well as the Tabi`oon (Followers) and the Followers of the Followers till the Day of Judgment.

- The author prays to Allah (swt) to reward all the `Ulama', who carried the Message of Allah (swt) and His Prophet (pbuh), and who transmitted it to the new generations.

- The author prays to Allah (swt) to reward his parents: his late father Al-Hajj Hussain Mustafa Sakr and his late mother Al-Hajjah Sara Ramadan Sakr for their sacrifices on their twelve children in general and to this author in specific. The author prays to Allah (swt) to reward the late brother of the author, Mr. Muhammad H. Sakr, for helping the author get his academic education, and his late brothers Mahmood H. Sakr, Mustafa H. Sakr, Farooq H. Sakr and Ibrahim H. Sakr for taking care of the author's responsibilities overseas.

- Special prayers go to the Shaikh of the author who taught him Islam, and trained him from childhood to practice its teachings: Shaikh Muhammad `Umar Da`ooq. May Allah (swt) be pleased with him.

- A special Du`aa' goes to Al-Shaheed Shaikh Hassan Khalid, the late Grand Mufti of Lebanon, who also had a great impact on the author's knowledge of Islam. May Allah (swt) bless his soul and grant him a place in Paradise.

---

1. swt: Subhanahu Wa Ta'ala (Glory be to Allah, and He is The High).
2. pbuh: Peace Be Upon Him (The Prophet).

- Special prayers and Du`aa' go to the many teachers, scholars and `Ulamaa' who were directly tutoring this author at the time of his youth. Through the efforts of Shaikh Muhammad `Umar Da'ooq, the following is a partial list of the teachers who taught this author: Dr. Mustafa Siba`ee; Shaikh Muhammad M. Al-Sawwaf; Dr. Muhammad Al-Zo`by; Shaikh Muhammad `Itani; Shaikh Muhammad M. Da`ooq; Shaikh Al-Fudail Al-Wartalani; Shaikh Muhammad `Abdel Kareem Al-Khattabi; Shaikh Malik Bennabi; Shaikh Faheem Abu`Ubeyh; Shaikh Muhammad Al-Shaal; Dr. Sa`eed Ramadan; Attorney `Abdel Hakeem `Abideen; Dr. Tawfic Houri; Shaikh Abu Salih Itani; Shaikh Hashim Daftardar Al-Madani; and the late Shaikh Abdul Badee` Sakr. May Allah (swt) bless them and reward them all.

- Our thanks and appreciation goes to Dr. M. Faseehuddin and all his family members for their contribution to this Foundation. A special thanks and appreciation go to Sister Dr. Sayeeda Sultana for donating on behalf of her mother, Mrs. Sultany Begum. May Allah (swt) reward Dr. Sultana, and may Allah (swt) bless her mother Sultany Begum. Moreover, we do thank Mr. and Mrs. Haitham Bundakji for their generosity to this Foundation at the time of needs. Ameen. Special thanks and appreciation go to Mr. Talat Radwan for helping this Foundation on behalf of his late father Mr. Mahmoud Radwan. In addition thanks to Sr. Nidhi Goomar for her support. May Allah (swt) bless them and be pleased with them. Moreover, we do thank Dr. M.F. Shoukfeh, M.D. and his family for their generous help to this Foundation.

- A final prayer is to the readers who took their precious time in reading this humble book: **Prepare Yourself and Speak.** May Allah (swt) bless them all. Allahumma Ameen.

Supplication

د عــا ء

God's Majesty Exalted

O Allah !   I seek refuge **in You** from anxiety and grief...
I seek refuge **in You** from incapacity and laziness.. and
I seek refuge **in You** from the overcoming of debts and
overpower of people...

O Allah !   I seek refuge **in You** from poverty except **to You,**...
from humiliation except **for You,** and from fear except
from You.

O Allah !   I seek refuge **in You** from stating false testimony... or
committing immorality, or provoking **You**; and
I seek refuge **in You** from the malice of the enemies,
and from enigmatic disease, and from the despair of
hope.

O Allah !   I seek refuge **in You** from the wicked people... from
the worries of the livelihood, and from the ill-nature..

O Allah !   **You are** the Mercy of the mercies, and **You are** the
Lord of the Universe.

Ya Allah!
Allahumma Ameen.

اللّٰهُمَّ

اللّٰهُمَّ إِنِّى أَعُوذُ بِكَ مِنَ الْهَمِّ وَالْحَزَنِ

وَأَعُوذُ بِكَ مِنَ الْعَجْزِ وَالْكَسَلِ

وَأَعُوذُ بِكَ مِنْ غَلَبَةِ الدَّيْنِ وَقَهْرِ الرِّجَالِ

اللّٰهُمَّ إِنِّى أَعُوذُ بِكَ مِنَ الْفَقْرِ إِلَّا إِلَيْكَ

وَمِنَ الذُّلِّ إِلَّا لَكَ وَمِنَ الْخَوْفِ إِلَّا مِنْكَ

وَأَعُوذُ بِكَ أَنْ أَقُولَ زُورًا أَوْ أُغْشَى فُجُورًا

أَوْ أَكُونَ بِكَ مَغْرُورًا وَأَعُوذُ بِكَ

مِنْ شَمَاتَةِ الْأَعْدَاءِ وَعُضَالِ الدَّاءِ

وَخَيْبَةِ الرَّجَاءِ اللّٰهُمَّ إِنِّى أَعُوذُ بِكَ

مِنْ شَرِّ الْخَلْقِ وَهَمِّ الرِّزْقِ وَسُوءِ الْخُلُقِ

يَا أَرْحَمَ الرَّاحِمِينَ وَيَا رَبَّ الْعَالَمِينَ

Section – One

PREPARATION

This book was supposed to be two separate books; one about Preparation to Speak and the other about Speeches for Different Occasions. However, we realized that a speaker, who is learning how to prepare a speech, also needs to know what topics to speak about for different occasions so that he may begin to actually formulate a speech. So the author decided to publish both topics, Prepare to Speak and Speeches for Different Occasions into this one book: ***Prepare Yourself and Speak.***

We all know that it is not easy to speak in public. It is also not easy to write or prepare a speech. This book is meant to be an inspiration and guidance to those who are asked to speak and those who are asked to prepare speeches on various topics. We have prepared a series of small speeches for different occasions. This series will offer many ideas to the speaker and help him prepare to speak to different groups for different occasions. The topics selected are of good interest to the speakers because they are very commonly used. Since it is impossible to compose a comprehensive list of topics ever needed to speak about on this planet earth, we selected some of the most popular, which can be used as a guideline to build on for all other topics.

Among the selected topics that were chosen by the author are the following: Before Speaking to non-Muslims; Hosting non-Muslims; Wrong Expectations; Salat Preparation; Friday Khutbah; Marriage Officiation; Ramadan Preparation; and Finally Preparation for Final Departure.

We hope and pray that many speakers, including Imams, Da`iyahs and others, will benefit from this humble work. We pray to Allah (swt) to accept this book from all of us. Ameen!

1

Chapter (1)   Introduction

I. General

During the sixties of the 20th century, I remember many Muslims couldn't attend the Friday (Jumu'a) prayer because there weren't enough Khateebs to deliver the Khutbah and lead the prayer (Salat). It was only the Mercy and Guidance of Allah that helped those few speakers who were asked, to deliver the Friday Khutbah every week. Since then, Praise Be to Allah (swt), a series of books were written, published and distributed within the USA and abroad, which benefitted many Muslims. This was a great blessing from Allah (swt) to all of us; the writers, those who used them, those who listened to them, and those who distributed them.

The titles of those books of Khutab are the following:

1.   Book of Khutab v.1

2.   Islamic Orations v.2

3.   Orations From the Pulpit v.3

4.   Chronicle of Khutab v.4

5.   Friday Khutab v.5

6.   Khutab Al-Masjid v.6

7.   Khutab From Mihrab v.7

8.   Manual of Friday Khutba

9.   Farewell Khutba of Prophet

Each of the books has between 20 - 40 Khutbahs. There are enough Khutbah's in these books that a Khateeb can make use of those Khutab's throughout the whole year. Each Khutbah has a different title and a slightly different approach of delivery. Many Imams have used these books as a guide to give the Friday Khutbah. Indeed, this is a blessing from Allah (swt).

2

We've started a series of training programs for those who wish to either become a Khateeb or those who wish to strengthen their public speaking skills. Such programs were attended by several friends and colleagues who wanted to know what the rules and regulations are for delivering a Friday Khutbah. They also wanted to know more about being an Imam in order to lead Salat (prayer). The participants attended the workshop for a period of 8 - 10 weeks. Each participant had to practice delivering a khutbah for 5 minutes in front of the class. The classmates were asked to advise the speaker on how to improve his speech and point out any mistakes. All the speeches were recorded so that the students could play back and listen to their own speeches, which would enable them to self assess their own mistakes. It was an excellent program and many benefited from it. A good number of Masjids participated in this program and have requested for this workshop to continue. We pray to Allah (swt) to accept our work. Ameen!

Later we got involved in writing books related to other topics such as Shari`ah; Allah (swt); Prophet Muhammad (pbuh); Family Values; Qur'an; Foods; Umrah and Hajj; Wisdom; inquiries; Du`aa'; Da'wah; Social Services; Sujood; Pillars of Islam; Adolescent Life; Understanding Islam; Islamic Listing; Knowledge; and many more. During that time in the sixties, we were very busy helping Muslims in various aspects of their lives, i.e., Counseling, Marriage, divorce, Eulogy, and many more.

II.   Before Accepting Invitations

1. If you are invited to speak at a function, try to find out as much information as possible regarding the purpose of the invitation, i.e. Jumu'ah, Salat, Spiritual Night, Qur'an Tafseer, Lecture, Workshop, Panel Discussion or some other reason.

2. Try to find out about the group and who the audience may be. For example, Religious affiliation, country of origin, some of their customs, habits, age group, and gender.

3. For example, if you are invited to give a Friday Khutbah, you'll want to find out about that particular Masjid and how they do things ahead of time. Since each Masjid is unique, you should ask some of the following questions:

   a. One Azan or two?

   b. Type of dress as an Imam.

   c. Is the Imam required to have a beard? If so, how long?

   d. Should the Khutbah be delivered in Arabic only, English only, or a combination of both Arabic and English?

   e. Do they require you give a talk next to the pulpit and then after the Azan is called you are to give Friday Khutbah in Arabic on the pulpit (Minbar)?

   f. Do they require you to carry a cane when you are giving a Friday Khutbah?

   g. Is it okay to raise your hands when you are making Du`aa' or should you refrain from raising your hands?

   h. How long should the Khutbah be?

   i. Is it okay to make Du`aa' aloud after the Salat is over?

   j. Do they expect you to make yourself available to the community after the Salat is over so the people may ask you questions or may discuss their problems with you?

    k.   Do they expect you to fundraise for the Masjid after the Salat is over? If so, you must be ready to do so or apologize to them?

4.   Prepare a series of Khutab on different topics. Make sure you have enough Ayat and Ahadith about the same subject matter.

5.   Prepare a series of talks on different subjects. Train yourself to speak for only (5) five minutes on a particular subject. Then try to speak for (10) ten minutes and then increase to 15, 20 and 25 minutes'. Try not to exceed your lecture more than that. Then challenge yourself and try to prepare a (1) minute speech. It is not as easy as you may think.

6.   Be polite. Don't force your ideas on others. Don't tell them what is right and what is wrong rather tell them what Allah (swt) and the Prophet (pbuh) told us.

7.   If they ask you what school of thought do you follow, tell them that I follow all the schools of thought. Whatever your local group or leaders prefer, I am for it.

8.   Yes! Go ahead and tell them in a friendly way; I am a Muslim first, last and forever. I am neither a Sunni nor a Shi'ah. I am not Shafi`ee...Hanafee...Maalikee...Hanbalee... or Ja'feree. I am just a Muslim, as was the Prophet (pbuh).

9.   If the Host asks you from which country are you from? Say, "I am from Islamistan, but I came originally from Kabristan!"

10. Be friendly to everyone. Associate yourself with the members of the Host Group. Keep smiling and be thankful to all for being invited to that event. Ask Allah to bless us all. Ameen!

Chapter (2)   Prepare Yourself To Be A Speaker

I. Introduction

Every Muslim is supposed to deliver the Message of Allah to as many people as possible. Everyone should understand that he is the Ambassador of Allah. Since, not every person can be a full time Da'iyah (speaker), some might be a part-time Da'iyah, and others might be a volunteer Da'iyah. However, Allah (swt) instructed the Muslim Ummah to recruit a group from within their society, and employ them as full-time Da'iyah to speak and to deliver the Message of Allah. In Surah Al-'Imran (The Family of 'Imran) Allah (swt) says the following:

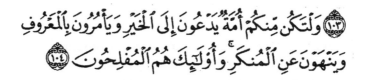

Let there arise out of you a band of people inviting to all that is good, enjoining what is right, and forbidding what is wrong: They are the ones to attain felicity. (Qur'an 3:104).

At the same time, Allah (swt) instructed the Muslims to recruit scholars to study the religion of Islam in order to teach the rest of the Muslim Ummah. As a reference, one may read Surah Al-Tawbah (Repentance), Ayah (9:122).

This means that a group of individuals from different parts of the world have to study Qur'an, Hadith, Sunnah, Sirah, Fiqh, Shari'ah, history, civilization, and the application of the religion of Islam to our current life. Those are the ones who might be considered Da'iyah. They are to be the teachers, the scholars, and the Ulamaa' of the Muslim Ummah.

6

II. Qualities of a Speaker

Whosoever should make Da'wah and speak in public has to remember that his conduct has to be a good example and a role-model for others to learn from. The following is a partial list of characteristics and qualities that a Da'iyah should have in order to be an effective speaker:

1. He should be a strong believer in the teachings of Islam utilizing all of the sources of Qur'an, Hadith, Sunnah, Sirah, Fiqh and the Shari'ah.

2. He should be a practicing Muslim, more so in his private life than in his public life.

3. He should be honest, sincere, and humble all at the same time.

4. He should study Islam from it sources but also seek guidance from Muslim scholars, Ulamaa' and professors.

5. He should memorize the Qur'an and the Hadith as much as possible.

6. He should know the culture, civilization, language, customs and habits of the people he has to speak to and deliver the Da'wah to. Know your audience at all times.

7. He should have a good degree of Taqwa (Righteousness), Wara' (Piety), Khashiya (Fear), and Khushoo' (Humbleness) toward Allah (swt).

8. He should learn how to have patience and perseverance while he is speaking and delivering Da'wah.

9. He should practice the concept of Shura (Consultation) with a group of knowledgeable Muslim scholars.

10. He should accept the advice and criticisms of his audience.

11. His services should be for the love of Allah. It should not be for the sake of money, position, or any titles.

12. He should recognize that Da'wah has no limit of time, effort, energy, knowledge, wisdom and money. You can never give enough.

13. Da'wah has no limit for its duration. A Muslim is to continue his Da'wah until he meets Allah (swt) on the Day of Judgment.

14. He should not ask nor seek recognition for his services.

15. He should try to live a modest life, and keep himself away from luxury or extravagancies.

16. He should use the approach of Targheeb much more than the methods of Tarheeb. This means that he should try to inspire encourage people and refrain from scaring people.

17. He should refrain from Bid'ah (Innovation), Kufr (Disbelief), Shirk (Association someone with Allah), Haram (Unlawful), or the like. These are very serious offenses in Islam.

18. He should refrain from giving titles to people by judging them. He has no right to judge people. The only One Who has that right is Allah (swt) and Allah (swt) alone.

19. The speaker should question himself every night before going to bed. He should ask himself whether his activities were for the love of Allah (swt) or not. He should plead his case to Allah (swt) to forgive him for his shortcomings and to reward him for any good services that he rendered.

20. Every now and then, he should conduct a self assessment of his activities and of his services. This evaluation should be done with other Da'iyah groups in order to be more effective.

21. There should be a system of coordination of activities with other speakers in the neighborhood. There should also be exchange programs among themselves.

III. Prepare Yourself

It should be stated here that the speaker has the responsibility to plan strategies before he starts speaking. The following is a partial list of things that a speaker needs to do before assuming any responsibility in the field of Da'wah:

1. He should define the Mission that he has to assume; otherwise he will be lost between East and West, or up and down. He would still be confused as to what he was supposed to do.

2. He should make sure that the mission is realistic as opposed to an unrealistic dream, hope or aspiration. The mission should be achievable if people are willing to work for it.

3. He should document his plans and strategies in a calendar or a planner; step-by-step and month-by-month.

4. He should understand the systems of the Government and the society with which he has to work with.

5. He should attend training programs, seminars and workshops in order to learn how to achieve his goals and learn how to better himself as a Da'iyah and a public speaker.

6. He should build an organization through which he gives advice, and he may have to receive instructions, advice, and possibly orders.

7. He should know how to recruit, delegate responsibilities, supervise, instruct, evaluate, advise and reward those who have achieved good results.

IV. Final Remarks

It should be stated here that the Da'iyah, as a speaker, is a mirror image of his community. He is the inheritor of the message from our Prophet (pbuh). And he must remember that he is the vice-gerent and a representative on behalf of Allah (swt) on this planet earth. Any wrong he does reflects badly primarily on his community and also on the rest of the Muslims around the world. Therefore, he should be conscientious about his role, personality, character, behavior and manners at all times. These adjectives and attributes are more important in the sight of Allah (swt) than any degree, prestige, title or position. We hope and pray that each and every Da'iyah will be cognizant of his situation in the community of people at large. Ameen.

There is no deity except Allah
Muhammad is the Messenger of Allah

Chapter (3)   Before Speaking to Muslims

I.   Introduction

As a Da'iyah and/or leader of the community, one of the most difficult things to deal with is the discourse between and amongst the Muslims. Today, throughout the world, you'll find many Muslims that are very difficult to deal with, to talk to and to resolve issues with. One of the reasons for this is that some Muslims feel that they are so knowledgeable in all aspects of Islamic life; Qur'an, Hadith, Sunnah, Sirah, Fiqh, Shari'ah, family, moral values, politics, education, bio-ethics, economics, banking, business, and many other social matters. Some would like to express their opinions because they have read one Ayah, one Haddith, or one chapter of a book. Others feel that they should give a Fatwa (verdict) for any question as if they are Mufti or Mujtahid.

It is not unusual to find, in some Muslim gatherings, a mad, outrageous individual who may act in a way as to disrupt the mobility of the congregation. Precautionary measures should be taken in advance, during and after the functions. There are many ways to handle such incidences; however, nothing will be resolved without patience, knowledge, wisdom, strong faith and sometimes firm action. This is why the proper leadership is imperative in a community due to the many problems that exist.

II.   Preparation

Prior to accepting a speaking engagement, one must prepare himself. The following is a partial list of recommendations:

1. Be honest and sincere with yourself and with Allah (swt).

2. Practice what you teach or preach, privately and publicly.

3. You should actively and continuously study Islam at different schools and at different levels.

11

4. Don't assume that **your** national customs, habits, and traditions are the true Islam. It's possible they may or may not be part of the teachings of Islam. You should check to make sure that none of them violate the teachings of Islam.

5. Be aware that Muslims are very different. Some are highly educated, while others are illiterate.

6. Do not assume that every Muslim who comes to the Masjid is a true believer and/or a practicing Muslim.

7. Try to memorize as many Ayat from the Qur'an as possible with the proper pronunciation and recitation.

8. Try to memorize as many Ahadith as possible with the proper pronunciation and reference to Sanad (proof), matn (text), and its recording book.

9. Try to study Sirah and matters of Fiqh from different schools of thought.

10. Acquaint yourself with the contemporary Muslim leaders, scholars, teachers, thinkers, speakers, movements, etc.

11. Acquaint yourself with the different Islamic Centers in your area as well as their activities and their leaders.

12. Don't assume that you're the only knowledgeable person in the crowd; don't assume that your opinion is the best opinion. There may be other opinions better than yours.

13. Children are very smart and there is a lot to be learned from them. Try to benefit from their wisdom.

14. Finally, don't assume that men are wiser than women! Correct your misunderstanding. There's a lot to learn from our female counterparts as well.

III. Beware Before Accepting Invitation

As an invited guest speaker you should be aware of the following:

1. You are the invited guest, not the host. So act like one.

2. Do not impose or force your ideas or your understanding of Islam on the local host who invited you. You may give them some recommendations; however, if they don't like any of them, don't worry! It is their problem.

3. Be cognizant that you'll encounter Muslims from many different countries with different customs, habits, and traditions.

4. Those same Muslims may adhere to different schools of thought. Some may be Shi`ah or Sunni Muslims.

5. Some Muslims may endorse a particular religious movement and some may have particular political views. Try to be neutral and adjust yourself to accommodate all these people with different views.

6. If you happen to belong to a movement, please do not publicize it at all; otherwise, you will find some opponents who will hate you and create discourse with you publicly. Keep your Bay'ah to yourself.

7. Don't be harsh! Be polite.

8. Don't argue! Try to absorb and reflect on other opinions.

9. Try to smile regularly. It makes people feel close to you. It is also a charity (sadaqah).

10. Be sociable and connected! Don't isolate yourself from the audience. Otherwise, no one will care for you.

11. Try not to give any Fatwa (verdict) or opinion. You are not a Mufti or Mujtahid. You are to discuss an issue from different points of views. Let the others decide for themselves. Request people to check with their inner hearts at a moment of devotion to Allah (swt).

IV. Final Remarks

Once it was said: If talking is from silver, silence is from gold. Since each person has two ears and one mouth, therefore, it is better to listen twice as much as you speak. If one has to speak, then you should remember the Ayah in Surah Al-Nisaa (The Women), whereby Allah (swt) says the following:

$$۞ لَّا خَيْرَ فِي كَثِيرٍ مِّن نَّجْوَىٰهُمْ إِلَّا مَنْ أَمَرَ بِصَدَقَةٍ$$
$$أَوْ مَعْرُوفٍ أَوْ إِصْلَٰحٍ بَيْنَ ٱلنَّاسِ ۚ وَمَن يَفْعَلْ ذَٰلِكَ$$
$$ٱبْتِغَآءَ مَرْضَاتِ ٱللَّهِ فَسَوْفَ نُؤْتِيهِ أَجْرًا عَظِيمًا ۝$$

In most of their secret talks, there is no good; but if one exhorts to a deed of charity or goodness or conciliation between people (secrecy is permissible): To him who does this, seeking the good pleasure of Allah (swt), We shall soon give a reward of the highest (value). (Qur'an 4:114).

Wisdom and **knowledge** are the key factors that will help you when talking and dealing with others. It is not **what** you want to say, but it is **how** you say it. It is to **whom** you want to talk, and **when** you should speak. The less you talk, the better it is for you

14

and for the audience. Khalifa Uthman Ibn `Affan ® once gave a Friday **Khutbah**. The whole sermon was one sentence:

أمّا بعد: أيّها الناس! أنتم بأمسّ الحاجة إلى إمام فعّال منكم إلى إمام قوّال.

O People! You are in need of an Imam of action rather than an Imam of talking.

We pray to Allah (swt) to bless all of us, and to guide us to the Straight Way (Assirat Al-Mustaqeem). Ameen!

Allah Al-Mu'min. Al-Muhaymin. Al-`Aziz. Al-Jabbar. Al-Mutakabbir

Chapter (4)   Hosting Non-Muslims

I.   Introduction

The following is a partial list of guidelines for those Muslims who wish to invite people of other faiths to their local mosques or Islamic centers. These guidelines are not all inclusive but rather recommendations. They've been extracted from past experiences. Those who may have had different experiences may use and share their own guidelines with their friends as to how to welcome people of other faiths. FYI- These recommendations are mainly for the members of the host community as well as the speaker.

II.   Before Attending

1. Invite some members from your own Muslim Community to attend the gathering so that they may help greet the guests.

2. Make sure that you cater food from a Muslim Halal food store.

3. Make sure to inquire about the dietary needs of the guests that are coming to your center. Some may be vegetarians; others may not drink coffee or tea. So be prepared to offer alternative food and drinks.

4. Try to find out the total number of the guest who are planning to visit your mosque and what is their religious affiliation.

5. Know your audience; it's important to know whether you're speaking to a group of college students, adults, youth or children. This also helps to plan ahead for the food.

III.   Before Presentation

1. Welcome the guests. Ask the members of the Muslim community to help you welcome the guests.

2. Let them socialize for 5-10 minutes and inform them about the facilities of your mosque or center in case anyone wants to make use of it.

3. Invite them for lunch or dinner with the local members of the Muslim Community. Tell them about the varieties of foods and drinks that have been prepared for them.

4. Let them socialize with other friends and guests before eating.

IV.   Presentation

1. Welcome them all again.

2. Let the Muslim community members introduce themselves.

3. Request the leader of the guests to say few words. He may request his members to introduce themselves.

4. Speak about Islam and Muslims; here are some topics:

    5 Pillars of Islam, 6 Pillars of Faith, Feasts and Festivities, Holidays, Islamic Calendar, Muslim diet, Early Muslim contributions to modern civilization, Present day Muslim contributions, Family values, Modesty, etc....

5. Inform them about the daily/weekly activities of your mosque.

6. At the end, give a chance for the guests to ask questions. Try to be objective and friendly. Don't be apologetic.

7. Allow some of the members of your community, especially the sisters, to say a few words.

8. Refrain from discussing the following topics:

    - Regional Politics
    - Proselytization

- Comparative religions unless in matters of commonalities
- Theology

V.   After the Presentation

1. Encourage them to ask questions.

2. Offer them the option to write their questions down on a piece of paper as opposed to asking in public in order to be discrete.

3. Offer them to take home any left over food.

4. Encourage them to take home any books/literature about Islam

VI.   Others

1. Try to make use of Visual aids.

2. Presentation structure (business-like with graphs, charts, etc.)

3. Keep your presentation short, sweet and within the time limits.

4. Thank your guests for coming. Encourage them to visit again.

5. Offer your services; offer your business card and contact info. Make yourself available for them anytime if they may have questions. You can send them a copy of the weekly Muslim community Newsletter via e-mail. Also, let them know that you would like to stay in touch.

6. Thank the audience/visitors as much as possible. If they wish to come again, encourage them to do so.

I. Introduction

As a speaker, you should expect to field many questions from the audience. You'll find that some wish to ask questions but in reality you'll find many who want to talk and express their own ideas. Instead of asking a question, they'll talk for so long that it feels like they are taking over the session. Others will ask questions that are totally unrelated to the subject matter of your lecture. As a speaker, you should not worry. The moderator is trained to handle such incidences. The moderator should announce to the audience that we are going to entertain questions related to the subject matter; no comments allowed. And if we have time at the end, we will allow comments from audience in addition to general questions that are unrelated to the subject matter.

II. Major Questions

Below is a list of the most popular topics that you could expect to get questions on from an audience:

1. Zabiha and Halal Foods.
2. Hijab for the Muslim women.
3. Music and singing.
4. Interest and mortgage.
5. Sunni and Shi'ah.
6. Marriage from non-Muslims.
7. Interfaith – is it Haram to deal or talk with them?
8. Whether a Muslim woman is allowed to come to the Masjid to pray or is it better for her to pray at home.
9. Is it true that the man is the boss in the family?
10. How come men inherit twice as much as women while women inherit half of what their brothers inherit?
11. Why do we need two women witnesses to a man's one?
12. Why can Muslim men marry more than one woman while women cannot marry more than one man?

13. In Salat, why do women have to pray behind the men?
14. Why can't a woman be an Imam of a community?
15. Different Jama'at. Which one is the best?

III. Learn More

From my humble experience, I'd like to advise everyone to learn about the philosophy, mission and activities of each Jama'ah before meeting, gathering or speaking to them. It is not possible to know them all so do your best. For the time being, here is a partial list of Islamic movements that you can familiarize yourself with.

1. Islamic Society of North America (ISNA)
2. Islamic Circle of North America (ICNA)
3. Muslim Arab Youth Association (MAYA)
4. Jama'at Tabligh
5. Hizb Al-Tahreer (California)
6. Habashi / Ahbash
7. Salafi Group
8. Sufi: Naqsh Bandi / Shazli / Rifaa'ee
9. Ikhwan Muslimoon:Muslim Brotherhood of Middle East
10. Jama'at Islami of Pakistan
11. Tanzeem Islami: Servants of Qur'an Society
12. Others and Others

IV. Final Remarks

Please! Do not judge any organization publicly. You don't know if someone in the audience belongs to one of the organizations. Inform the audience that we are not here to publicize or attack any organization. Don't endorse or criticize any school of thought. Remind the audience to focus our talk on the Topic at hand. For questions about other topics, offer your phone number, e-mail and and/or website for those who wish to contact you later. May Allah (swt) bless you and reward you.

Chapter (6)   Wrong Expectations

I.   Introduction

Most people expect to receive the best in this world and in the hereafter. Often, speakers are required to travel from city to city to give lectures and participate in panel discussions, seminars, and workshops, etc. Some have to travel when they are invited to give a Friday Khutbah. Usually speakers will anticipate that their trip will go smoothly and good comes their way. In the next section, the author wishes to make the speaker aware of the possible adversities that he may encounter while on the journey or as an invited guest. In doing so, the author wishes to prepare the speakers to have adverse expectations versus positive expectations. This type of thinking will help prepare the speaker mentally to better deal with whatever calamities may come his way. This will also give him immunity against all types of false expectations and help him to make Ihtisab (anticipation & expectation from Allah).

II.   What To Expect

1. As a guest, you may have to pay your travel expenses and you may even be asked to give a donation to the local society. Consider yourself fortunate if they do otherwise.

2. If travelling by plane, expect delays and to be stranded at the airport for sometime. Be prepared to manage yourself.

3. Don't assume that you are the only invited speaker. There may be others sharing the panel with you. Or you may be alternating from one session to another.

4. Expect last minute changes; the local community may change the time of your speech as well as the title of your speech at the very last minute. You need to be prepared to accommodate the changes.

5. Expect to be confronted, challenged, blamed and criticized publicly by some crazy, ignorant person from the audience. Try to be calm and cool and absorb what he is saying.

6. During the Friday Khutbah, expect to be challenged by someone who has no respect for the Khutbah or the prayer.

7. As a traveler, someone may ask you to lead Salat. Expect that another person may shout out and say, "you cannot be Imam because you are a traveler".

8. Don't expect anyone to thank you or show you any form of gratitude; not for your lecture, for your travels, for your hard work or for your participation.

9. Don't expect to receive a gift, a souvenir, a letter of appreciation or even a welcoming smile.

10. You should expect some people to spread some type of rumor about you without any reason at all.

11. If an honorarium is offered to you, expect the local Muslims to feel jealous. Expect to be criticized and accused for accepting such a thing when you are making Da'wah for the sake of Allah (swt).

12. After receiving the honorarium from a university, the local student body may ask you to sign the check and pass it over to them. They will do this publicly to embarrass you. Don't worry.

13. Expect uncomfortable lodging accommodations. You were told that the local people reserved a local hotel room for you. In order to save money, they cancelled the hotel room and put you up with a family that you don't know.

14. After the function is over, everyone is excited and happy; however, you'll find yourself feeling stranded and alone with no one to give you a ride to your hotel room. You'll feel used because they got what they wanted from you and no one will accommodate you. Be prepared to handle it.

15. When leaving, you may find that you don't have a ride from the hotel to the airport as promised. Not only will you have to pay a taxi to get to the airport but you find that you'll also have to pay the hotel for the night you stayed. Don't worry! This is your account with Allah (swt).

16. You may find yourself returning frequently to the same community because the local people like you very much. Accordingly, each wants to have you as a guest at their local homes. As a result, your coat may end up at one house, your suit case at another house, your briefcase at a third house, and yourself at a fourth house. Upon leaving town the next day, you have to collect your items from all the different places. Please don't complain!

III. Final Remarks

One has to realize that the journeys of life are not easy. That's why helping one another is an absolute must. The rewards you receive on this planet may not be satisfactory. The only true reward is from Allah (swt) on the Day of Judgment. Our recommendations to the speakers would be to take it easy and don't expect good treatment from any one. You are a Da'iyah and your job is to convey the Message of Allah to everyone, just like the Prophets did. Remember how all the previous Prophets and Messengers were mistreated by their own local people. Take it easy and thank Allah (swt) that your trial isn't as hard as theirs. Remember, your reward is with Allah (swt) Insha Allah . Ameen!

Chapter (7)   Salat Preparation

I. Introduction

Muslims are commanded by Allah to pray to Him (5) five times daily. This is an obligation that every Muslim must fulfill. For the men, they are required to congregate and pray every Salat Jumu`ah (Friday prayer) in a Masjid. Other required prayers are Salat of Eid-ul-Fitr, after fasting in the month of Ramadan and Salat Eid-ul-Adha, Pilgrimage sacrifice- during Hajj. There are many other types of Salat as well.

Salat in Islam is not a supplication but it includes a variety of requirements. Performance salat is another item that one has to learn the prerequisites, and how to do them. At the end of each salat there is a special Du`aa' (supplication) that one has to say and to do.

II. Prerequisites

One of the prerequisites (requirements) is Intention and then Cleanliness. A Muslim has to make sure that his body is clean, his undergarments are clean, and his outer clothing is clean as well. He has to make Ablution (Wudoo'): how to start and how to finish the requirements of Ablution (Wudoo'). It is incumbent upon oneself when he prepares himself for Salat to fulfill these requirements (thorough cleanliness). He has to realize that Allah (swt) does know everything, and He records everything as well.

A Muslim has to learn how to pray and must do so 5 times a day. Zuhr (Noon) and 'Asr (afternoon) are performed in silent prayers, whereas the remaining 3 Salat (prayers) may be done either vocally or silently. In each ruk'a, one must recite Surah Al-Fatiha plus any other Surah of their choice. One should learn how to recite the Qur'an during salat with the original Arabic Language. He should learn how to perform the physical rituals of prayers (salat), Qiyam (standing), Rukoo' (bowing forward),

Sujood (prostration), and the Tahiyyaat (sitting while saluting the Prophet-pbuh). Moreover, one should learn the direction of (Qibla) so that the Salat is directed towards Ka'bah (Makkah).

III. As an Imam

1. One has to study and learn from Muslim scholars (silent and vocal ones) how to be an Imam and how to lead the Friday (Jumu`ah) congregational prayers.

2. One should learn how to recite the Qur'an with proper pronunciation and with a melodic voice. The Imam leads the congregations while behind him are the believers who follow the Imam during the prayer.

3. One has to train himself to be an Imam with his family first before being an Imam in Public. Then he may try to lead Salat for students before leading Salat in a Masjid. Before leading Salat, he should request another scholar to watch him lead Salat and then to advise him how to be better.

IV. Final Remarks

Learning how to lead Salat is very important. What's even more essential is practicing to be an Imam under the supervision of another Imam or scholar. Improving our intentions with Allah should also be a top priority before doing anything else. One has to realize that Salat is a communication directly with Allah so we must try and perfect this act of worship. It is also a Mi'raj; going up and up to Allah, and putting this world behind us while we're in the state of Salat (prayer). We pray that Allah (swt) will guide us how to practice Salat, and how to lead salat properly. Ameen!

Chapter (8) Before Accepting Friday Khutbah

I. General

1. Try to find out about the group: Religious affiliation, country of origin, some of their customs, habits, age group, and gender.

2. For example, if you are invited to give Friday Khutbah, try to ask some of these questions:

    *   One Azan or two?

    *   Type of dress required as an Imam?

    *   Is the Imam required to have a beard? If so, how long?

    *   Should the Khutbah be in Arabic or should it be delivered in a combination of Arabic and English?

    *   Do they require that you give a talk next to the pulpit and then after the Azan is called you can give the Friday Khutbah in Arabic on the pulpit (Minbar)?

    *   Do they require you to carry a cane when you are giving a Friday Khutbah?

    *   Is it OK to raise your hands when you are making Du`aa?

    *   How long should the Khutbah be?

    *   Is it okay to make Du`aa' out loud after the Salat is over?

    *   Do they expect you to stay after Salat so that people may ask you questions and discuss their problems with you?

    *   After Salat, do they expect you to raise money for that Masjid? If yes, you need to be ready otherwise, you'll have to apologize to them?

3. Prepare a series of Khutbahs on different topics. Make sure you have enough Ayat and Hadith about the same subject.

4. Bring with you the gown, cap and Tarha. Put them on before entering the Masjid.

5. Don't go by yourself. Take someone with you so that you'll have company with you on the way there and on the way back.

6. If someone gives you a ride, offer them a gift for taking you. May Allah bless you all!

II. Final Remarks

1. Be informed! It is always better to know your audience and your environment before you get there.

2. So prepare yourself and be prepared to adjust to any situation before going to any Masjid to deliver the Friday Khutbah.

3. Be thankful to all who are present at the Jumu'ah prayer especially those who invited you to give the Friday Khutbah.

4. Be grateful to Allah (swt) Who is directing and guiding you on how to be an Imam and a Khateeb. Delivering the Message of Allah (swt) is the climax of any other service.

5. Make Du'aa' of thanks and appreciation within you to Allah (swt). We'll also pray for you. Ameen!

Chapter (9)   Friday Khutbah (Part 1) / Khateeb

I.   Introduction

Dear Muslims

Assalamu `Alaikum

Although it could be quite challenging to give a lecture to Muslims and non- Muslims alike, it is more difficult to be an Imam and to lead the Salat (prayer). The Salat of Noon (Zuhr) and of After-noon (`Asr) are easier because they done silently. Maghrib, Isha, and Fajr prayers are performed vocally. One has to be careful what to recite, how to recite and for how long to recite. This has to be even more so perfected during the Friday Khutbah and Salat. Preparation and getting it right is one of the most sensitive tasks of the Friday Congregational prayer.

One must know how to quote the Qu'ranic verses in the original language of the Qu'ran and with the proper pronunciation. One needs to know how to start a Khutbah and how to end it. He should also know how to make Du`aa' in the language of the Qur'an. One has to be careful how to pronounce the Ayat and the Hadith with a proper accent. The following is some advice on how to prepare Khutbah:

II.   Khateeb

In order to be a Khateeb, one has to attend workshops as well as to take a courses on how to give a Friday Khutbah. The following is a summary of what a person should do:

1.   Attend a workshop for several sessions.

2.   Take a course from some religious scholars.

3.   Try to practice how to read and recite Qur'an.

4.   Try to practice how to read Hadith properly.

5. Try to practice how to make Du`aa' in Arabic.

6. In the workshop, you should be able to practice giving a small khutbah in front of the other students.

7. Listen to their advice on how to improve your Khutbah.

8. By the way: The khutbah should not be more than five minutes including the introduction and the Du`aa'.

9. Remember when you want to be a Khateeb, you must recognize the different cultures and backgrounds of the Muslims attending the Khutbah. Some might be Shafi`ee, Hanafee, Maalikee, Hanbalee, or Shi`ee.

10. As a Khateeb, one should wear an `Abaaya or proper dress. He should have a beard and wear a cap on his head and sometimes with a Tarha.

11. The Khutbah should not be longer than 15 or 20 minutes, otherwise people will get tired and bored.

12. Try to learn the art of speaking, otherwise your speech or Khutbah it will sound monotonous.

13. The title of the Khutbah should be clear. The Ayat and the Hadith should reflect the title of the Khutbah.

14. Remember; the audience is looking & listening to you.

15. Try not to read word-for-word what you have written except for Qur'anic Ayah and Hadith.

16. Try to look at the congregation while giving a Khutbah. They'll feel more connected to you.

17. Try to use hand gestures and facial expressions while giving the Khutbah. The audience will feel close to you.

18. The Friday Khutbah is composed of two Khutbahs; the first one should be about the topic of discussion and the second one should be for making Du`aa' (supplication).

19. If you think you're ready to start giving Friday Khutbahs, please don't try to start with a community. Instead go to a college or university first and give the Kutbah to the students there.

20. Try to repeat giving Khutbahs at different Muslim students Associations (MSA).

21. If you think you are doing well then you can move to a small community and then later to a larger community.

22. Try to move around from Masjid to Masjid. Try not to give a Khutbah to the same group of Muslims week-after-week. The more you get around, the more successful you'll find yourself.

III.   Final Remarks

To be a Khateeb for Friday Congregational prayer is the climax of Da'wah. The Khateeb represents Prophet Muhammad (pbuh) in delivering the Khutbah. Friday is a Holy and Sacred day for Muslims; it's the most important day of the week. Muslims come together to pray and to refresh their memory of Islamic teachings. It is also a means to meet and get to know one another & improve their friendly relationships. Friday is the day whereby Muslims try to help each other and donate money to the needy families. Therefore, the Khateeb should take all of this into consideration and act accordingly. Ameen!

Chapter (10)   Friday Khutbah (Part 2) / Imam

I.   General

To be an Imam for the Friday Congregational Salat is not easy. It is a special Salat (noon prayer) composed of two (2) Khutbahs and a two Rakat prayer to be recited vocally. Normally the noon prayer is recited silently. But on Friday, since it is a holy day, the Imam will lead the prayer vocally and should know exactly how to quote the Ayat from the sacred Qur'an. Further, for the Khutbah, he should know how to quote the Hadith on behalf of the Prophet (pbuh) in the original Arabic Language. His Arabic recitation and pronunciation should also be clear and appropriate.

II. Imam

The Imam who leads the congregation in Salat must realize the following:

1. Attend a training program before assuming the responsibility.

2. Practice reading and reciting verses from the Qur'an vocally at home before delivering the Khutbah and Friday Salat.

3. Make sure that the first Rak`ah is longer than the second one.

4. In the first Rak`ah you may choose to recite any Surah or Ayat from the Qur'an.  However, in the second Rak`ah, you must recite a verses or Surah from the Qur'an that sequentially follows the first one you recited. For example,

    In the first Rak'ah, if after Surah Al-Fatiha you recite Surah Al-Falaq, then in the second Rak'ah you can't recite Surah Al-Kaafiroon. You can only recite Surah Al-Naas.

5. Before reciting Qur'an, you should silently glorify Allah as follows:
    - Subhaanakat Laahumma Wa Be Hamdika

- Tabaarakass Smuka WaTa'aala Jadduka
- Wa Laa Ilaaha Ghairuka

6. Then it is better to say A'oozu and Bismi before reciting Surah Al-Fatiha, as follows:

   - A'oozu Billahi Minash-Shaitaanir Rajeem
   - Bismil Laahir Rahmaanir Raheem

7. Try to recite the Qur'an with a melodic voice; of course, using the rules and regulations of pronunciation and recitation.

8. In every Rak'ah there are seven (7) positions. The Imam should move slowly-slowly so that the followers will be able to follow him without missing any of the positions.

9. As a visitor of another Masjid, the Imam should ask whether or not its OK to make Du'aa' publicly after the Salat is over.

10. While leading Salat, it is recommended that you put your hands on top of one another while standing and reciting Qur'an.

11. While leading Salat, you may raise your hands at every movement when you say Allahu Akbar.

12. Beware that some Masajid don't like the Imam to make Du'aa' publicly while others expect the Imam to do so. Don't worry!

13. Some Masajid want the Imam to give Friday Khutbah only in Arabic. This means, prior to the Khutbah, you'll have to give a talk in English or a local language. Then you'll go up to the pulpit and give the Khutbah in Arabic. These groups usually require the Imam to wear a beard and dress in a gown, Abaya, cap, and Tarha over cap. As an Imam you should always be prepared to present yourself in a way that accommodates the different needs of the community leaders.

14. Other Masajid/communities may not have strict requirements as the one mentioned in #13. They don't require the Imam to wear a gown, Abaya, cap, tarha, or a beard. The Imam is free to dress in normal work clothes, i.e. a suit and necktie. He can use the English language as much as possible. He may demonstrate that he is a moderate American Imam through his appearance. This is OK too.

15. If a Mufti happened to be in the Masjid, the Khateeb may request that the Mufti lead the Salat after the Khutbah is done.

16. If the Khateeb has to sit on chair to pray due to medical problems in his legs, then he has the right to ask another person to lead the Salat and be the Imam.

17. Many Masajid like to make announcements immediately after the Salat is over. They don't need to make special Du`aa'. That is Okay too!

III. Final Remarks

A Khateeb is a Khateeb, who delivers the Khutbah but an Imam is an Imam, who leads the Salat. For each one of them there are rules and regulations. One has to know the differences and act accordingly. The best and most important position to assume is to be both a Khateeb and an Imam. You should be grateful that Allah (swt) selected you to be a Khateeb and an Imam for the Friday Salat. The more thankful you are to Allah (swt), the more Allah (swt) will guide you and bless you. Ameen!

I. General

Dear Muslims

Assalamu `Alaikum

One of the responsibilities that come with being a Da'iyah is the privilege to officiate Muslim marriages. The Da'iyah must learn how to officiate a Muslim marriage and must know how to implement its rules and regulations. There are general and specific concepts related to the family. The following are some general concepts that the Da'iyah should be aware of before assuming the responsibility of officiating any marriage:

1. The family is the cornerstone and the foundation of a social, cultural and religious structure in the society.

2. God created man from a single soul and made the spouse a mate for him.

3. Then God created all of us in a large number. So we should fear, respect, and appreciate Allah (swt) for His creation.

4. From among His signs are mates (spouses), who have been created, so that they may dwell together in tranquility. To fulfill this covenant, Allah (swt) has granted compassion, love, sympathy, concern and mercy between the two spouses.

5. Allah (swt) has given all of the above so that we may think, ponder, contemplate and reflect.

6. Sexual relationship before marriage isn't allowed just as extra-marital relationships aren't permissible after they are married.

7. Marriage Life in Islam is a form of worship, just as praying, fasting and other spiritual rituals. Once you marry, you are considered to have fulfilled half of your religion.

8. Marriage extends beyond the newlywed couple to include the extended families of both sides. The family members of each side (bride and groom) become blood relatives to one another.

9. Love between the couple starts after marriage. If love starts before the marriage, then it will definitely stop after marriage.

10. During the courtship (Khitbah), before the marriage ceremony (Nikah), the two individuals should get to know each other under the supervision of their parents or guardians. There shouldn't be any privacy between them during this time.

II.   Rules for Officiating Marriage

1. A gentleman seeking to get married should look for a girl who is compassionate, pious, tender and bashful.

2. For an official marriage to take place, a marriage ceremony must be performed whereby there needs to be at least two (2) witnesses present and preferably from their blood relatives.

3. The "mahr" or dowry is to be offered by the groom to the bride. This denotes a commitment by the groom to the bride that he will take responsibility for the family.

4. After the marriage ceremony has been performed, it is recommended that a "Waleemah" be offered for the newlywed couple. A Waleemah is a dinner where friends and family are invited to celebrate & share in the joy of the newlywed couple.

5. It is recommended that Khitbah (courtship), Nikah (marriage) and Walimah ceremony be announced publicly so everyone will know. The marriage isn't just a union between the two.

6. Marriage has both worldly and heavenly benefits all at once.

7. Marriage helps people live healthy, stable lives; morally, socially, culturally, spiritually, economically and biologically.

III. Specifics

It was the Sunnah (Tradition) of the Prophet (pbuh) to deliver Khutbahtun Nikah during the wedding ceremony. The meaning of the word Khutbahtun Nikah is a sermon or speech that is given just before the marriage vows are exchanged. The Imam (Ma'zoon), who is officiating the marriage for the young couple, should give a religious sermon to the people attending the marriage.

The Imam should recite to the audience a few verses from the Qur'an and a few quotations of Hadith. He should remind the couple of their obligations to each other as husband and wife. He should also encourage the young adults to get married as soon as they possibly can.

After reading and exchanging the vows, the Imam should pray for their happiness. Then he can sign the official marriage papers along with the guardian (wakeel) and the two witnesses.

It is recommended that the pre-marriage agreement should be signed and notarized too. The agreed upon dowry (Mahr) should be recorded in the state as well as in the Masjid.

IV. Final Remarks

Know that you are fortunate to be invited to officiate a marriage. In doing so, you'll realize the different customs and habits of Muslims from different parts of the world. Be courteous and friendly to all. This is not the time to tell the families about what's Halal and Haram. Talk about Targheeb but not Tarheeb. Encourage them and thank them for their effort of officiating an Islamic Marriage in a non-Muslim country such as USA.

I. Introduction

Dear Muslims

Assalamu `Alaikum

Fasting during the month of Ramadan is the fourth pillar of Islam. All Muslims are obligated to fast unless they are excused due to illness or travel. In Surah Al-Baqarah (The Cow), Allah (swt) says the following about fasting:

۞ يَٰٓأَيُّهَا ٱلَّذِينَ ءَامَنُوا۟ كُتِبَ
عَلَيْكُمُ ٱلصِّيَامُ كَمَا كُتِبَ عَلَى ٱلَّذِينَ مِن قَبْلِكُمْ
لَعَلَّكُمْ تَتَّقُونَ ۞ أَيَّامًا مَّعْدُودَٰتٍ فَمَن كَانَ مِنكُم
مَّرِيضًا أَوْ عَلَىٰ سَفَرٍ فَعِدَّةٌ مِّنْ أَيَّامٍ أُخَرَ وَعَلَى ٱلَّذِينَ
يُطِيقُونَهُ فِدْيَةٌ طَعَامُ مِسْكِينٍ فَمَن تَطَوَّعَ خَيْرًا فَهُوَ خَيْرٌ
لَّهُ وَأَن تَصُومُوا۟ خَيْرٌ لَّكُمْ إِن كُنتُمْ تَعْلَمُونَ ۞

O you who believe! Fasting is prescribed to you as it was prescribed to those before you, that you may (learn) self-restraint. (Fasting for a fixed number of days; but if any of you is ill, or on a journey, the prescribed number (should be made up) from days later. For those who can do it (with hardship), is a ransom, the feeding of one that is indigent, but he that will give more, of his own free will, it is better for him. And it is better for you that you fast, if you only knew. (2:183-184)

There are rules and regulations for fasting as well as for being excused from the fast. Muslims fast as a sign of obedience to Allah (swt) and in return, they will earn blessings from Allah (swt), the Creator of the Universe. In addition to earning rewards from Allah (swt), there are many other benefits that come with fasting; i.e. social, economic, spiritual, cultural, psychological, medical, health and many more.

There are many other types of fasting outside of the teachings of Islam. The people of the Book (Christians and Jews) were also ordained to fast by Allah (swt). They were also asked to fast as a matter of obedience to Allah (swt).

Wise people in early history of mankind used to fast for forty days before they offered any wisdom or gave advice. That meant that if a person wanted to become wiser, then he/she would fast for a number of days either continuously, from dawn to sunset, or from time to time. Further, fasting was prescribed as a remedy for those who were sick along with some other health remedies.

II Benefits of Fasting

A. General Benefits

By fasting the proper way, one will achieve better health. The Prophet Muhammad (pbuh) once mentioned:

Fast and you will attain Health.

Here are some of the major health benefits of fasting:

1. Purification of the Body

2. Reduction of Body Weight

3. Looking Younger

4. Purity and Clarity of the Brain

5. Rejuvenation of the Body

B. Spiritual Benefits

In as much as fasting has medical benefits it also has spiritual benefits as well. Among the many benefits, one of the main benefits of fasting is forgiveness from Allah (swt) for all the mistakes that we've made throughout the whole year. In order to receive such gifts from Allah (swt), one has to fast in Ramadan, pray the five daily prayers, pray Taraweeh prayers, read Qur'an, listen to the recitation of Qur'an, observe the Night of Power (Lailatul Qadr), and so on. The following is a partial list of benefits that one can achieve from Fasting:

1. Forgiveness from Allah (swt)

2. Fasting During Ramadan Has Many Blessings

3. Another Level of Forgiveness

4. Blessings of the Night of Power

5. Blessings of Sahoor

II Final Remarks

Fasting is a one of the key rituals that will bring happiness to people. One can achieve real peace by fasting intermittently throughout the year and for the month of Ramadan. This routine can also prevent sickness in their life. Allah (swt) prescribed fasting for all mankind from the days of Adam and Eve until the Day of Judgment and He made it a pillar of Islam. For those who obey Allah (swt) by fasting according to Qur'an and Sunnah, they will be rewarded a healthy and happy life. On the Day of

Judgment, those who fasted will have a better way of life than the rest of the people in Paradise.

During the fasting period, people should eat less than normal. They should reduce their weight and change their normal life routine from being monotonous. They should spend their nights doing extra spiritual rituals such as Taraweeh prayers, Tahajjud, Nafila and Qyima Al-Lail. They should read the Qur'an and listen to its recitation by others. This may cause them to sleep less but they'll earn more rewards from Allah (swt) and as a result they'll feel happy. These rituals will help rid some of Depression, Loneliness, and a Dull Life that some may be living. By overcoming the monotony of a dull routine and life miseries, one can achieve a happy and healthy life. It is easy to write or talk about the process and procedures of our life style during the month of Fasting. However, it's more important to try to practice them and to enjoy life the way Allah (swt) wanted us to enjoy it.

We pray for each honest and sincere faithful believer to enjoy fasting in the month of Ramadan and to receive the physical, biological, medical and spiritual rewards of it. Ameen!

No one will touch it except the purifiers

Chapter (13) Preparation for Departure

I. Introduction

Dear Muslims

Assalamu `Alaikum

The subject of my talk is about Preparing Ourselves To Leave This World To Go To The Next World: The Eternal Life. We are all going to die and no one will stay or live eternally on this planet. In Surah Al-Zumar (The Companies), Allah (swt) says:

Surely you shall die and they (too) shall surely die. [Qur'an 39:30]

The Qur'an clearly states that each person will taste death with its bitterness or sweetness. That will depend upon how bad or good the person was in his life. Allah (swt) says in Surah Al-'Imran (Family of `Imran) the following:

Every soul shall taste of death, and you shall only be paid fully reward on the resurrection day; then whoever is removed far away from the fire and is made to enter paradise, he indeed has attained the object; and the life of this world is nothing but a provision of vanities. [Qur'an 3:185]

II Local Departure

Dear Muslims

There are several ways and methods for departures; some are by our own will, such as preparing ourselves to leave for Hajj or to visit another country in the world. Another method of departure could be by force such as refugees who are forced out of their own countries. Others could be deported from their country because they are being suspected or illegal. Hence, these people try to prepare themselves as much as possible. They take with them whatever they can, i.e. money, commodities, supplies, etc. They may have to get a passport, visa, inoculation, air ticket and so on. All these preparations are meant for a short trip. However, if one should leave this planet and go out of the orbit forever, then he definitely has to prepare himself properly and well in advance.

III. Eternal Departure

Dear Muslims

Our discussion here is the preparation for the Eternal Departure from this world to the next world. Once we depart this world we'll be stationed in different places until we reach our final destination of either Heaven or Hell. First we'll have to live in the grave for a long period of time. We'll wait there until we're called up for the Day of Assembly, followed by the Day of Judgment. Then each of us has to walk on the Sirat Al-Mustaqeem. We have to zoom towards Hell and to the 'Araf station before being taken to Paradise. In each and every place, we will be interrogated, checked and cross-examined.

Dear Muslims

Our departure from this world is going to be without our permission. None of us will know when, where or even how we'll leave. Allah (swt) says the following in Surah Luqman:

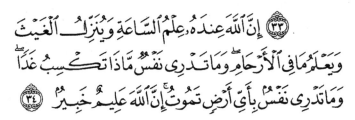

...Nor does any one know what it is that he will earn on the morrow; nor does any one know in what land he is to die. Verily, with Allah (swt) is full knowledge and He is acquainted (with all things). (31:34)

IV Preparation

Dear Muslims

Since it is a fact that we're all going to die, then the question therefore is: How we should prepare ourselves before it is too late. The answer to such a question could be summarized as follows:

1. Everyone should make istighfar and tawbah on a daily basis. This means that you should repent to Allah (swt) and ask for His forgiveness daily. Our beloved Prophet (pbuh) used to do this 70 - 100 times a day.

2. One should feel sorry for doing wrong as well as for not performing or doing the right thing.

3. One should pledge to Allah (swt) that you'll take initiative to do good to all. Some of the major favors that you may have to perform are:

    a. Sadaqah or charity; some of which are related to money, while others may be related to social, religious and educational matters.

    b. Bring people together and help them to live in peace and harmony.

4. Be a good example for others. This cannot be achieved unless you are on good terms with Allah (swt). This means that you need to practice what's obligatory, according to Islamic rules and regulations, and have the intentions to please Allah (swt).

5. Ask forgiveness from Allah (swt) for your mistakes as well as for your shortcomings. You have to remember that Allah (swt) will forgive you only after you forgive others.

V. Hurry! Don't wait

Dear Muslims

You may say now, "what are we going to do"? The answer is: Don't wait! Don't procrastinate and say tomorrow I will repent and go to Hajj and be a good Muslim. Please don't delay your decision to come back to Allah (swt)! If you delay, it only makes you lose the golden opportunity to be accepted by Allah (swt).

Remember my dear Muslims that our beloved Prophet (pbuh) demanded from us to take the initiative and do good deeds before it is too late. In one Hadith, Abu Hurairah reported that the Prophet said:

١٦٩٢ ـ عن أبي هريرة رضي الله عنه أن رسول الله صلى الله عليه وسلم ،
قال : « بَادِرُوا بِالأَعْمَالِ سَبْعاً ، هَلْ تَنْتَظِرُونَ إلاَّ فَقْراً مُنْسِياً،
أَوْ غِنىً مُطْغِياً ، أَوْ مَرَضاً مُفْسِداً ، أَوْ هَرَماً مُفْنِداً (١) أَوْ مَوْتاً مُجْهِزاً (٢)
أَوِ الدَّجَّالَ فَشَرُّ غَائِبٍ يُنْتَظَرَ ، أَوِ السَّاعَةَ فَالسَّاعَةُ أَدْهَى وَأَمَرُّ! »
رَوَاهُ التِّرْمِذِيُّ وَقَالَ : حَدِيثٌ حَسَنٌ .

Undertake the seven deeds: Are you waiting for the poverty which will make you to forget; or a transgressing wealth; or an impaired sickness; or a wear-out age; or a ready made death; or the impostor Al-Dajjal – an absent evil is waiting; or the hour of resurrection!? Indeed, the hour of resurrection is worst, bitter and severe. [Narrated by Abu Hurairah; Tarmazi].

VI. Final Remarks

Dear Muslims

Let us take the initiative to do good before we die, and let us pray to Allah (swt) requesting Him to forgive us and to keep us guided until we meet Him. Ameen, ya Rabbal 'Alameen!

Let us ask Allah (swt) for His Guidance, Mercy, Blessings and Forgiveness. Ameen!

And be good to parents

Section –Two

SPEECHES

I. Introduction

In the previous Section, we have offered a series of advice to the speakers that will help them before they start to speak. We hope and pray that the speaker will be trained very well before he accepts an invitation to speak. Recently, we realized that many people have been invited to speak about topics in which they did not have enough information from Qur'an and Hadith to prepare or deliver a good speech. A good number have been asked to speak about several different types of Islamic occasions. We've decided to help them by preparing speeches on different topics. Hence, why we felt it necessary to write a book that will include a series of talks for different occasions such as:

1.	Prophet's Birthday	9.	Umrah and Hajj
2.	Marriage	10.	Ameen Celebration
3.	Waleemah	11.	Hifzul Qur'an
4.	`Aqeeqah	12.	Ayati Kareemah
5.	Graduation	13.	Mother's Day
6	Eulogy	14.	Thanksgiving
7.	Sickness	15.	Others
8.	Tragedy		

The speeches are simple and short, not to exceed 10 minutes. Some may choose to make their speeches shorter or longer or some may choose to speak about an entirely different topic. He may also include more information, from Qur'an or Hadith. The speaker must use wisdom and know what to say and for how long to speak.

We pray to Allah (swt) that many Muslims will benefit from this series of Lectures and Speeches. As a result, Muslims will have a better understanding of the teachings of Islam through Qur'an, Hadith and the Seerah of the Prophet. Ameen!

Chapter (14)   Pledge Of Allegiance (Part 1)

I.   Introduction

Dear Muslims

Assalamu `Alaikum

Let me introduce the subject with an Ayah from the Qur'an regarding the Pledge of Allegiance. In Surah Fussilat, Allah (swt) says:

إِنَّ ٱلَّذِينَ قَالُواْ رَبُّنَا ٱللَّهُ ثُمَّ ٱسۡتَقَـٰمُواْ تَتَنَزَّلُ عَلَيۡهِمُ
ٱلۡمَلَـٰٓئِكَةُ أَلَّا تَخَافُواْ وَلَا تَحۡزَنُواْ وَأَبۡشِرُواْ بِٱلۡجَنَّةِ
ٱلَّتِي كُنتُمۡ تُوعَدُونَ ۝ نَحۡنُ أَوۡلِيَآؤُكُمۡ فِي ٱلۡحَيَوٰةِ
ٱلدُّنۡيَا وَفِي ٱلۡءَاخِرَةِ وَلَكُمۡ فِيهَا مَا تَشۡتَهِىٓ أَنفُسُكُمۡ
وَلَكُمۡ فِيهَا مَا تَدَّعُونَ ۝ نُزُلًا مِّنۡ غَفُورٍ رَّحِيمٍ ۝

In the case of those who say, "Our Lord is Allah", and further, stand straight and steadfast, the angels descend on them (from time to time): "Fear you not!" (They suggest), "Nor Grieve!" We are your Protectors in this life and in the Hereafter; therein shall you have all that you desire; therein shall you have all that you ask for! "A hospitable gift from One Oft-Forgiving, Most Merciful" (41:30-32)

Every country in the world has a Pledge of Allegiance to either its flag, its President, its king, its leader, its constitution, or its political party. Even Muslim countries nowadays have such a pledge. Each country's pledge has different versions and texts; some are general while others are specific. Most of the pledges are secular and devoid of a religious commitment. Some pledges verbally state that they have a commitment to God, to their president and to their country all at the same time. A loyal citizen is expected to defend all three even if he is to die for their sake. Unfortunately, not all Presidents are practicing Muslims so its possible that a president may demand from his citizens to commit wrong actions. Those who are loyal to their president will fulfill his demands even if it means that they have to die in order to defend their leader.

II. Muslim Loyalty

For a Muslim, his loyalty, allegiance, and obedience first and foremost are to Allah (swt). His commitment is to Allah (swt). The first pillar of Islam is a declaration of a Muslim's pledge of allegiance, a vow, a commitment, and an oath to Allah (swt). This type of declaration is the Creed of Tawheed (Oneness of God). It is called the Shahadah and it states as follows:

أَشْهَدُ أَنْ لاَ إِلَهَ إِلاَّ اللهُ

I bear witness that there is no one worthy of worship except the only one God (Allah)

و أَشهد أن محمداً عبْدُهُ وَرَسوُلْهُ

and I bear witness that Muhammad (pbuh) is the last Messenger of Allah to all of humanity till the Day of Judgment

Dear Muslims

Prophet Muhammad (pbuh) stayed thirteen years in Makkah preaching to his followers the concept of Tawheed and the concept of a Pledge of Allegiance to Allah (swt). When we say "Allahu

Akbar," we are reminded that Allah (swt) is bigger and better than anything else in the universe. A Muslim is continuously reminded of the concept of Allahu Akbar during:

1. Azan

2. Iqamah

3. The two calls (Azan and Iqamah)

4. All movements during the 5 daily prayers

5. During Tashahhud

III. Final Remarks

Dear Believers

A Muslim, whose loyalty is to Allah (swt), will say, "I am a Muslim first, last and forever. I have submitted myself, my hopes, my wishes and my aspirations all to Allah (swt). I have accepted Allah (swt) as my sole Creator, Sustainer, and Lord of the Universe. I have accepted the Qur'an to be the words of Allah (swt) and I will abide by the teachings of the Qur'an. I will follow the Qur'an in its totality even if it is against my wishes, my desires, and my lusts. I have accepted the Prophet Muhammad (pbuh) as the one who has interpreted, explained and lived the teachings of Qur'an. He is the last, the final and the most important Prophet and Messenger of Allah (swt) till the Day of Judgment. I will also acknowledge those from amongst the Muslims who have submitted themselves to Allah (swt) as leaders of our Ummah".

Chapter (15) Pledge Of Allegiance (Part 2)

I. Introduction

Dear Muslims

Assalamu `Alaikum

Our pledge of allegiance is to Allah (swt) and Allah (swt) Alone. For those who take Allah (swt) as their Lord and obey Him publicly and privately, vocally and silently in our intentions, Allah (swt) will be their Waliy (Protector). It is said in the Qur'an that

1. Allah is the Waliy of the Believers
2. Allah is the Waliy of the Muttaqeen (those who are pious)

Since Allah (swt) is The Waliy and He is the Waliy of the believers, then it is our duty to rely on Him. Allah (swt) is the One whom we worship and whom we ask for help. One of our pledges of allegiance is found in Surah Al-Fatiha which we read several times in our five daily prayers (Salat). The pledge is as follows:

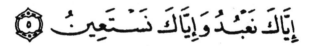

To you (O Allah)! We worship, and from You (O Allah)! We ask for help. (Qur'an 1:5)

Dear Muslims

Allah (swt) demanded that we submit to Him, obey Him, take Him as our Waliy (Protector), and take His Prophet Muhammad (pbuh) and the believers as Awliya' (leaders). In this respect, Allah (swt) says in the Qur'an in Surah Al-Ma'idah (The Table Spread):

﴿ ٥٤ ﴾ إِنَّمَا وَلِيُّكُمُ ٱللَّهُ وَرَسُولُهُۥ وَٱلَّذِينَ ءَامَنُوا ٱلَّذِينَ
يُقِيمُونَ ٱلصَّلَوٰةَ وَيُؤْتُونَ ٱلزَّكَوٰةَ وَهُمْ رَٰكِعُونَ ﴿ ٥٥ ﴾ وَمَن يَتَوَلَّ ٱللَّهَ
وَرَسُولَهُۥ وَٱلَّذِينَ ءَامَنُوا فَإِنَّ حِزْبَ ٱللَّهِ هُمُ ٱلْغَٰلِبُونَ ﴿ ٥٦ ﴾

...Your (real) friends are (no less than) Allah, His Messenger, and the (Fellowship Of) believers - those who establish regular prayers and pay Zakat and they bow down humbly (in worship). As to those who turn (for friendship) to Allah, His Messenger, and the (Fellowship Of) believers - it is The Fellowship of Allah that must certainly triumph. (5:55-56)

Remember, my dear Muslims that Allah (swt) will protect you and take care of you in this world and in the Hereafter. Allah (swt) reminded us in Surah Yunus by saying:

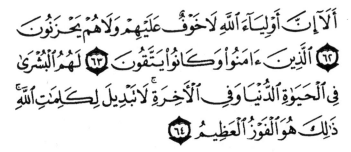

Behold! Verily on the friends of Allah there is no fear, nor shall they grieve; those who believe and (constantly) guard against evil - For them are Glad Tidings, In the life of the present And in the Hereafter: No change can there be In the words of Allah. This is indeed The supreme Felicity. (10:62-64)

Our Prophet Muhammad (pbuh) informed us of the following:

٣٣٧ – وَعَنْ أَبِي ذَرٍّ ، رَضِيَ اللهُ عنهُ . قَالَ ۤ قَالَ : رَسُولُ اللهِ . صلَّى اللهُ عليهِ وسلَّمَ : « قَدْ أَفْلَحَ مَنْ أَخْلَصَ قَلْبَهُ لِلإِيمَانِ، وَجَعَلَ قَلْبَهُ سَلِيماً ، وَلِسَانَهُ صَادِقاً ، ونفسَهُ مطمئنَّةً ، وخَليقتَهُ مستقيمَةً » . (ابن حبان)

51

Indeed he succeeded, the one who purified his heart for faith; who made his heart clean (and pure); (who made) his tongue truthful; who made his soul at peace; and who made his life activities straight forward. (Narrated by Abu Zarr Al-Ghaffari (raa), and reported by Ibn Habban

II. Final Remarks

Dear Muslims

This subject can best be summarized by reciting the following Ayah, in Surah Al-An'am (The Cattle):

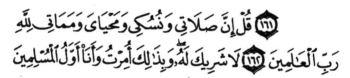

Say: "Truly, my prayer, And my service of sacrifice, My life and my death, are (all) for Allah, The Cherisher of the Worlds; No partner hath He: This am I commanded, And I am the first Of those who bow To His Will." (6:162-163)

Dear Muslims

We pray to Allah (swt) to accept our pledge of allegiance; and we pray that our pledge is pure for His love. Let us make a Du`aa' ask Allah for His forgiveness and guidance. Ameen.

رَبَّنَآءَاتِنَافِى ٱلدُّنْيَا
حَسَنَةً وَفِى ٱلْأَخِرَةِ حَسَنَةً وَقِنَاعَذَابَ ٱلنَّارِ ﴿٢٠١﴾

Our Lord! Give us good in this world and good in the Hereafter. And save us from the torment of Fire!

I. Introduction

Dear Muslims

Assalamu `Alaikum

Thank you for inviting me to speak about Loyalty and Allegiance to Allah (swt).   It is a very important topic indeed. Muslims should always put their trust in Allah (swt) first, last and forever.   For those who follow leaders that do not obey Allah (swt), they are indeed the losers.   Allah (swt) warned us not to take the disbelievers as our protectors and our leaders.   In Surah Al-Mumtahinah (The Woman to be Examined), Allah says:

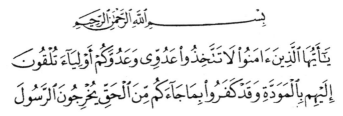

O you who believe! Take not My enemies and yours as friends (or protectors) - offering them (Your) love, even though They have rejected the Truth That has come to you. (60:1)

Allah (swt) also informed us that those who have taken the disbelievers as their leaders have made the devils as their protectors.   In Surah Al-`Araf (The Height) Allah says:

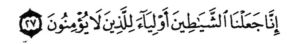

We made Satans friends (only) to those without faith. (7:27)

In the same Surah, Allah (swt) says about those who take the evil ones as their protectors, that they are misguided.

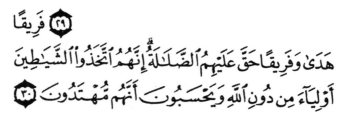

...In that they took the Satans, in preference to Allah, for their friends And protectors, and think That they receive guidance. (7:30)

In Surah Al-Baqarah (The Cow), Allah (swt) informs us that those who take the evil ones as their leaders are considered to be disbelievers and their leaders are tyrant dictators who bring people from light to darkness. Their final abode will be in Hellfire. Allah (swt) says in this regard, the following:

اَللَّهُ وَلِيُّ ٱلَّذِينَ ءَامَنُواْ يُخْرِجُهُم مِّنَ ٱلظُّلُمَٰتِ إِلَى ٱلنُّورِ وَٱلَّذِينَ كَفَرُوٓاْ أَوْلِيَآؤُهُمُ ٱلطَّٰغُوتُ يُخْرِجُونَهُم مِّنَ ٱلنُّورِ إِلَى ٱلظُّلُمَٰتِ أُوْلَٰٓئِكَ أَصْحَٰبُ ٱلنَّارِ هُمْ فِيهَا خَٰلِدُونَ ۝

...Of those Who reject faith the patrons Are the evil ones: from light They will lead them forth Into the depths of darkness. They will be Companions Of the fire, to dwell therein (Forever). (2:257)

Allah (swt) informed us that He is The Waliy. It is He who is our Protector, our Leader, our Creator, our Sustainer, our Hope, our Aspiration, and our Expectation. Allah (swt) tells us in Surah Al-Shura (Consultation) that He is The Protector (The Waliy):

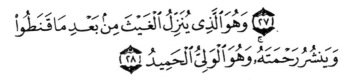

...And He (Allah) is the Protector, worthy of all praise. (42:28)

II. Final Remarks

Dear Muslim

An individual who dies in the cause for his president, his leader, his country, or for a party usually gets a medallion on his grave.   His name is mentioned among the many who have sacrificed their lives for the sake of their boss.   Those who lose their lives for worldly affairs will get nothing for it in the hereafter. However, those who have lost their lives and their loyalty is to Allah (swt), they will receive the blessings of Allah (swt) both in this world and in the hereafter.

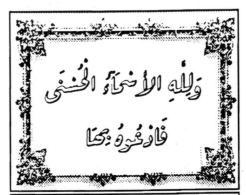

"The Most beautiful names belong to Allah: so call on Him by them."
(Qur'an 7:180)

Chapter (17)   Significance of Friday

I. Introduction

Dear Muslims

Assalamu `Alaikum

My talk today is about the **Significance of Friday**. Friday is a very important day in the sight of Allah (Subhanahu Wa Ta'ala). Allah (swt) has ordered us to gather together on Friday for a congregational prayer to demonstrate our obedience, allegiance and loyalty to Him.

My dear Muslims, before I elaborate on the importance and the significance of Friday, let me remind you of what Allah (swt) says in the Qur'an in Surah Al-Jumu'ah (Friday) about the Friday Congregational Prayer. Allah (swt) says:

يَـٰٓأَيُّهَا ٱلَّذِينَ ءَامَنُوٓاْ إِذَا نُودِىَ لِلصَّلَوٰةِ مِن يَوۡمِ ٱلۡجُمُعَةِ فَٱسۡعَوۡاْ إِلَىٰ ذِكۡرِ ٱللَّهِ وَذَرُواْ ٱلۡبَيۡعَ ذَٰلِكُمۡ خَيۡرٌ لَّكُمۡ إِن كُنتُمۡ تَعۡلَمُونَ ۞ فَإِذَا قُضِيَتِ ٱلصَّلَوٰةُ فَٱنتَشِرُواْ فِى ٱلۡأَرۡضِ وَٱبۡتَغُواْ مِن فَضۡلِ ٱللَّهِ وَٱذۡكُرُواْ ٱللَّهَ كَثِيرًا لَّعَلَّكُمۡ تُفۡلِحُونَ ۞ وَإِذَا رَأَوۡاْ تِجَٰرَةً أَوۡ لَهۡوًا ٱنفَضُّوٓاْ إِلَيۡهَا وَتَرَكُوكَ قَآئِمًا قُلۡ مَا عِندَ ٱللَّهِ خَيۡرٌ مِّنَ ٱللَّهۡوِ وَمِنَ ٱلتِّجَٰرَةِ وَٱللَّهُ خَيۡرُ ٱلرَّٰزِقِينَ ۞

O you who believe! When the call is proclaimed to prayer on Friday (The Day of Assembly), Hasten earnestly to the Remembrance of Allah, and leave off Business (and traffic): That is best for you if you but knew! And when the Prayer is finished, then you may disperse through the land, and seek of the Bounty of

Allah: and remember Allah frequently that you may prosper. But when they see some bargain or some pastime, they disperse headlong to it, and leave you standing. Say: that which Allah has is better than any pastime or bargain! And Allah is the Best to provide (for all needs.) (62:9-11)

II. Significance

Dear Believers

In order to elaborate more about the significance of Friday, let me mention and enumerate the following items to you:

1. Allah (swt) created Adam on Friday

2. Allah (swt) made Adam and Eve descend from the Heaven to the earth on Friday.

3. Adam died on Friday.

4. The Day of Judgment will take place on Friday.

5. Friday is considered to be the Master of all other days.

6. Allah (swt) considers Friday to be more important than Eid-ul-Fitr and Eid-ul-Adha

7. On Friday, there is one hour when the doors of Heaven are wide open and the Du`aa' (Supplication) is accepted.

8. Everything in the Universe has respect and fear for the day of Friday, including angels, heavens, earth, winds, mountains and seas.

9. Friday is more important than any other day of the week.

Dear Muslims

These nine items have been summarized by the Prophet Muhammad (pbuh) when he said:

سَيِّدُ الأَيَّامِ يَوْمُ الْجُمُعَةِ وَأَعْظَمُهَا عِنْدَ اللَّهِ تَعَالَى،

وَأَعْظَمُ عِنْدَ اللَّهِ تَعَالَى مِنْ يَوْمِ الْفِطْرِ وَيَوْمِ الأَضْحَى،

وَفِيهِ خَمْسُ خِلَالٍ:

خَلَقَ اللَّهُ عَزَّ وَجَلَّ فِيهِ آدَمَ عَلَيْهِ السَّلَامُ

وَأَهْبَطَ اللَّهُ تَعَالَى فِيهِ آدَمَ إِلَى الأَرْضِ

وَفِيهِ تَوَفَّى اللَّهُ تَعَالَى آدَمَ

وَفِيهِ سَاعَةٌ لَا يَسْأَلُ الْعَبْدُ فِيهَا شَيْئًا إِلَّا أَتَاهُ

اللَّهُ تَعَالَى إِيَّاهُ مَالَمْ يَسْأَلْ حَرَامًا، وَفِيهِ تَقُومُ

السَّاعَةُ؛

مَامِنْ مَلَكٍ مُقَرَّبٍ وَلَا سَمَاءٍ وَلَا أَرْضٍ وَلَا رِيَاحٍ وَلَا

جِبَالٍ وَلَا بَحْرٍ إِلَّا هُنَّ يُشْفِقْنَ مِنْ يَوْمِ الْجُمُعَةِ

Master of the days is Friday; it is mightier in the sight of Allah (swt) than any other day; it is even mightier than Eid-ul Fitr and Eid ul-Adha. There are five important incidences that occurred on Friday: Allah created Adam on Friday; and on Friday Allah (swt) made Adam to die; during this holy day there is one hour whereby if a person makes Du`aa' to ask Allah (swt), He will answer his Du`aa' unless what he asked for is haram; the Day of Judgment will takes place on

58

this day, and angels who are closed in proximity, heavens, earth, winds, mountains and sea all indeed are scared of the day of Friday.

10. Friday is a festive (Eid) day for Muslims. They congregate to pray together as a community. They listen to the Khutbah in which the Imam discusses certain pertinent topics relevant to the Muslim Ummah. He must inspire and motivate while reminding them of their duties and responsibilities which will bring them closer to Allah (swt).

11. On Fridays, Muslims are advised to read Surah Kahf (The Cave). In doing so, they will be forgiven by Allah (swt) for the whole week. They will also receive light from Allah (swt) which will extend from earth to the upper heavens. This light will shine for them on the Day of Judgment.

12. When Muslims come to Friday Congregational Prayer with good intentions, Allah (swt) will give them blessings and rewards according to their time of arrival.

13. On Fridays, Muslims are encouraged to give greetings and Salat unto Prophet Muhammad (pbuh). In this is a great reward from Allah (swt).

14. Friday is a day of cleanliness. Muslims are commanded to take a shower on Friday. Hence, they will be rewarded accordingly. Muslims are to put on their best clothes and dresses for salat.

III. Final Remarks

Dear Muslims

Friday is a very important day in our life and we should observe it with great fervor. We should anxiously await its arrival and we should increase our Du`aa' for someone in absentia.

O Allah (swt) bless us because we need your help and Mercy. O Allah (swt) forgive us because we are sinners. Let us ask Allah forgiveness. Ameen.

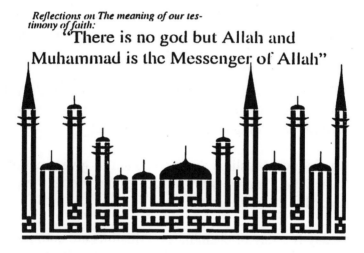

Reflections on The meaning of our testimony of faith:
"There is no god but Allah and Muhammad is the Messenger of Allah"

I. General

Dear Muslims

Assalamu `Alaikum

The topic of my discussion today is about the Blessings of the month of Zul-Hijjah. Allah (swt) says the following in the Qur'an in Surah Al-Tawbah regarding the four sacred months:

$$\text{إِنَّ عِدَّةَ ٱلشُّهُورِ عِندَ ٱللَّهِ ٱثْنَا عَشَرَ}$$
$$\text{شَهْرًا فِى كِتَٰبِ ٱللَّهِ يَوْمَ خَلَقَ ٱلسَّمَٰوَٰتِ وَٱلْأَرْضَ}$$
$$\text{مِنْهَآ أَرْبَعَةٌ حُرُمٌ ذَٰلِكَ ٱلدِّينُ ٱلْقَيِّمُ فَلَا تَظْلِمُوا فِيهِنَّ}$$
$$\text{أَنفُسَكُمْ وَقَٰتِلُوا ٱلْمُشْرِكِينَ كَآفَّةً كَمَا}$$
$$\text{يُقَٰتِلُونَكُمْ كَآفَّةً وَٱعْلَمُوٓا أَنَّ ٱللَّهَ مَعَ ٱلْمُتَّقِينَ ﴿٣٦﴾}$$

"The number of months in the sight of Allah is twelve (in a year) - So ordained by Him The day He created The heavens and the earth; of them four are sacred: that is the straight Religion.... (9:36)

These four months mentioned in this Ayah are Zul-Qi'dah, Zul-Hijjah, Muharram and Rajab.

II. Significance

Dear Muslims

The month of Zul-Hijjah is a sacred and a blessed month. Because of its importance, Allah (swt) has sworn in the first ten days of this month, by saying in Surah Al-Fajr (The Daybreak):

By the Dawn; By the ten Nights; By the Even and Odd (contrasted) and by the Night when it passes away - Is there (not) in these an adjuration (or evidence) for those who understand. (89:1-3)

Dear Muslims

It has been mentioned in the book of Ibn Khathir that Al-Fajr is referred to the Dawn prayer for the Eid; that the phrase "Layalin Ashr" are the ten nights of Zul-Hijjah; that the word "Al-Shafa'" is the day of Sacrifice; and that "Al-Witr" is referred to the 9th day of Zul- Hijjah which is the Day of Arafa.

In this respect, it is reported that the Prophet (pbuh) said:

حَدَّثَنِى حُرَّ بْنُ نُعَيْمٍ عَنْ أَبِى الزُّبَيْرِ عَنْ جَابِرٍ عَنِ النَّبِيِّ صَلَّى اللّٰهُ عَلَيهِ وَسَلَّمَ قَالَ :

«إِنَّ الـعَشْرَ عَشْرُ الأَضْحَى ،وَالوِتْرَ يَوْمُ عَرَفَةَ ،وَالشَّفْعُ يَوْمُ النَّحْرِ»

وراه النسائى

Narrated by Jabir that the Prophet said:

Indeed, the ten are the ten (days) of Al-Adha (sacrifice), the odd (witr) is the day of Arafa, and the Shafa' (even) is the day of Sacrifice.

62

III. Blessings

Dear Muslims

There are many blessings during the month of Zul-Hijjah. The following is a list of some:

1. During this month the performance of Hajj is prescribed.
2. The performance of Hajj is of great significance to the individual as well as to the Muslim Ummah as a whole. It is the fifth pillar in Islam.
3. Great benefits are gained by those who perform Hajj such as:
    a. Purification from Sins
    b. Fulfilling the fifth pillar of Islam
    c. To get to know one another
    d. To solve many of the problems of the Muslim world.
4. Fasting: Each day you fast in the first ten days of Zul-Hijjah is equivalent to fasting one whole year.
5. Night worship: Each night of worship is equivalent to Lailatul Qadr.

The Hadith of the Prophet (pbuh) narrated by Abu Hurairah:

No one day is liked by Allah (swt) more than those of the ten days of Zul-Hijjah where (people) worship Him. Each fasting day is equivalent to one year fasting; and each Qiyam (night prayer) is equivalent to Lailatul Qadr.

6. Doing good work in the way of Allah (swt) and for the love of Allah (swt) is equal to the reward of Jihad.
7. Doing good deeds in these ten days is more liked by Allah (swt) than anything else; it is liked even more than Jihad in the way of Allah (swt).

8. Due to the great blessings of the first ten days, Muslims are asked to say Tahlil, Takbir and Tahmid, i.e. to say the creed, to say God is the Greatest and to praise God.

9. Fasting the day of Arafa:

    Whoever fasts the day of Arafa (the day before the Eid), Allah (swt) will forgive him for two years: one year before and one year to come; and if you fast the day of Ashura, Allah (swt) forgives one past year.

    For a pilgrim who is on Hajj, it is prohibited for him to fast on the day of Arafa.

IV. Final Remarks

Dear Muslims

There are many more blessings for the month of Zul-Hijjah. However, due to the shortage of time, we'll speak about them during the next session or Khutbah. Meanwhile, let's pray and ask Allah (swt) to bless all the Muslims all over the world during this Blessed Month of Zul-Hijjah. Ameen!

And He (Allah) has power over all things.
(Qur'an, 11:4)

I.   Introduction

Dear Muslims

Assalamu `Alaikum

Today, I'd like to continue our talk from last week about the Blessings of the month of Zul-Hijjah. I'd like to mention and include some more Blessings that Allah (swt) has given us during this month. You should know that Allah (swt) blesses the Muslims so many times throughout the whole year. You should try to learn about the many blessings that Allah (swt) has for us. However, now I'd like to focus on the many blessings that we have in the month of Zul-Hijjah. We hope and pray that Muslims will practice many rituals so as to receive the blessings of Allah (swt). Ameen!

II.   Some Blessings

1. Forgiveness for the Pilgrims: whoever performs Hajj, with good intentions and absence of wrong doings, will be forgiven for all his sins. They'll return back home as if he/she is a brand new human being.

2. The Day of Arafa itself is so blessed that Allah (swt) releases people from the Hellfire due its significance.

3. The reward for the pilgrim is paradise: when a person performs Hajj, his utmost reward is paradise itself.

4. Life insurance and assurance by Allah (swt): if a person dies while performing Hajj, he will go to paradise. If they return back home, then they'll come back as a winner and with blessings.

5. Spending money while on Hajj is similar to that spent in the battle field; and equal to 700 times.

6. The Sacrifice of animals on Eid-ul-Adha must be shared with and distributed to the poor, needy, friends, neighbors, relatives, and the members of your family.

7. Visit the cemetery and make Du`aa' for the deceased Muslims. This will also help remind you that you'll spend the next phase of your life in another world, the grave.

8. Visit Muslim friends and give gifts.

9. The performance of the pilgrimage during Hajj is accepted by Allah (swt) if the Muslim has paid for his Hajj with halal money and earnings.

10. While on Hajj, the pilgrim is given the privilege to ask forgiveness for others. It is reported:

Allah (swt) forgives the pilgrim and the person whom the pilgrim has asked forgiveness for. Ibn Khuzaimah

III. Final Remarks

It is recommended that we try our best to benefit from the privileges and blessings that are given to us in the month of Zul-Hijjah. This month offers many golden opportunities to us and I hope that we'll be able to capitalize on the opportunity to be close to Allah (swt).

We pray to Allah (swt) to accept our deeds and our good intentions.

Dear Muslims

Let us ask Allah (swt) guidance and forgiveness. Ameen!

I. General

Dear Brothers and Sisters

Assalamu `Alaikum

We thank Allah (swt) for creating us as human beings. We thank Him for the Faith He put in our hearts. We thank Him for the knowledge he gave us and for the eloquence He gave us in our tongue and our speech. I also want to thank all of you for attending this session, and all those who organized this program.

Dear Brothers and Sisters

Many Muslims have just performed Hajj without knowing enough about its rules and regulations. With good intentions but without planning or preparation, they have made a series of mistakes in their performance of the Hajj. For every mistake that is made, they must give recompense (Kaffarah). Similarly, if we make a mistake in on of our prayers, we have to make Sujood Al-Sahu (prostration for making a mistake). Or if we break our Wudoo', then we have to repeat the Wudoo' and Salat, and so on.

Many of us did not know how to prepare ourselves properly for Hajj, i.e. spiritually, psychologically, socially, culturally, economically, etc. We did not have enough time to learn all what is needed to perform the Hajj properly. A large number of Muslims were shocked when they arrived in Mecca. Even those who went with their own groups were shocked from what they saw and experienced. Their worldly expectations were not met accordingly. But the real problem is that we were unprepared for the Hajj. We must prepare ourselves long in advance for this once-in-a-lifetime journey to Allah's (swt) Holy City that He has selected for us to visit in order to fulfill and complete our Faith as Muslims.

II. Preparation for Hajj

The following is a partial list of things that we should keep in mind in order to prepare ourselves for Hajj:

A. General Requirements

1. The good intention to make Hajj

2. Halal money

3. Ihram dress

4. Valid passport

5. Air ticket: it should be a round-trip ticket

6. Vaccination

7. Visa: It should be given from the country of origin. In the US, you have to be either a citizen or have a green card.

8. If you are born in the U.S.A., you should have a certificate that shows you are Muslim, especially if your name doesn't appear to be Muslim and even if you were born to a Muslim family.

9. If you are female, you must be accompanied by a Mahram, who is usually a male member of your immediate family such as your father, husband, son or brother.

B. Recommendations

1. Please do not go by yourself. Try to go with groups who have made arrangements with a Mu'allim (teacher). He will guide you spiritually throughout the trip.

2. Attend a workshop at your local community center in order to better understand the rules and regulations and the day-to-day activities of how to perform the rituals of Hajj.

3. Before you go, make sure you make a will and leave a documented copy with an authorized person who will know how to execute it in case you die in Mecca and never return. The family should know how to handle the family affairs in the case of your death.

4. Take travelers checks instead of cash. Only carry a limited amount of cash. If you lose your travelers checks, you can recover your money.

5. You should safeguard your money in safety pockets and a safety belt. Never leave your money in the hotel. Always keep it with you at all times.

6. Don't take food, water, or any cooking utensils. The Holy Cities have all the necessary accommodations to live easily.

7. Although there is plenty of medicine there and the pharmacists usually give medicine without physician's prescription, make sure you take your medication that you need, especially if you have a sickness.

8. If this is your first trip, please don't take any of your children with you. It will be tough for them and for you too.

9. Children should be taken for 'Umrah first during December or summer vacation. They will enjoy the trip and they will have good memories about the Holy Cities.

10. Take guide books on Hajj and 'Umrah. Read them before you go. Ask your guide to explain anything you do not understand.

11. Take a Qur'an with you. Keep yourself busy by reading the Qur'an. Enjoy talking to Allah (swt) while reading the Qur'an.

12. Take with you a book titled, <u>Al-Du'aa' Al-Mustajab (The Accepted Du'aa')</u>. Read and make all varieties of Du'aa'.

13. Continue to make Takbeer (Allahu Akbar); Tahleel (La Ilaha Illa Allah); Tahmeed (Al-Hamdu Lillah); Tassbeeh (Subhan Allah)...etc.

14. Continue to recite Talbiyah (Labbaika Allahumma Labbaik).

15. Remember, this is a spiritual journey! Don't worry about what other Muslims are doing wrong. You should only be concerned with yourself and whether or not Allah (swt) will accept your Hajj.

16. The purpose of the journey is to perform Hajj; and the Eid is called Eid-ul-Adha (Feast of Sacrifice). Try to sacrifice your time, your effort, your money and your knowledge in helping other Muslims who are there with you.

17. Try to be as patient as possible. Makkah is over crowded with millions of people gathered around the Ka'bah all trying to make Tawaf and Sa'iy. Try not to push anyone and try to move with the flow of traffic. There will be some pilgrims who are ignorant and don't respect Sha'aa-irr (rituals) of Hajj. They may push and shove people without any respect to others. Take it easy and say, "La Hawla Wa laa Quwata Illa Billah".

18. When you arrive at Jeddah Airport, you'll be tired and exhausted. You'll immediately want to either go to the hotel or go to perform 'Umrah before the Hajj begins. However, you won't be able to do so until the authorities have processed your visa. You'll have to be patient though because there are a few hundred thousand individuals like yourself who just arrived that day. So in the meantime, sit back, relax, read Qur'an,

make Zikr, Tassbeeh, Istighfar, and Talbiyah. Also try to extend your help to others within and outside your own group.

19. The weather may be too hot for you. Drink a lot of water. You may need to use salt-tablets as well due to perspiration without noticing it. Try to be in the shade as much as possible. You may not feel the heat of the sun but it's possible to get sun stroke or meningitis which could lead to a sudden death.

20. Stay away from heavy crowds. You may not know when someone may push you or others. Many stampedes have occurred during Hajj and many have died as a result. At that time it would be difficult to stand up on your feet. Someone might step over you, and it would be difficult to stand up.

21. If you take your wife along, you may throw the pebbles in the Jamarat (throwing pebbles) at the three Shaitans on her behalf during your stay of three days in Mina. These days, the stay in Mina is better than it was before.

22. Some may be confronted with situations that many individuals will not know how to handle themselves. They'll need someone to help them, guide them, or offer advice. Try to be the first ONE to offer your services. You can also be their translator if they don't speak English, Arabic or Urdu, etc....

23. When you are at Mina, living in the tents, try to identify the location and direction of your tent so that you'll know how to return back to your tent. All tents look alike so it's easy to get confused and get lost. Once you are lost, it is very difficult to find your way back to your tent.

24. If you are unable to sacrifice an animal on the day of Eid, give the money to someone to do it for you on your behalf. The Organization of Islamic Conference (OIC), which represents

the whole Muslim sovereign states, will assume the responsibility on your behalf. The meat is then frozen and later distributed to the different parts of the Muslim world.

III. Final Remarks

Dear Brothers and Sisters

We pray to Allah (swt) to bless all those who are planning to perform Hajj. We should make Du`aa' for them so that they will be blessed by Allah (swt). Ameen!

Qur'an (24:35)

| Chapter (21) | Speech For Umrah |

I. Introduction

Muslims are encouraged to go to Makkah and make Umrah. There are specific rules and regulations on how to perform Umrah. Before arriving in Jeddah, Saudi Arabia, the following rules must be observed:

1. Take a shower for cleanliness

2. Put on 2 pieces of cloth (like towels for men) and praying two Rak'ah

3. Declare and make the intention to perform Umrah when you reach Meeqaat

4. Once you enter the Masjid of Ka'bah, you are required to make Tawaf around the Ka'bah (circle around the Ka'bah counter clockwise) seven (7) times

5. Pray two Rak'ah and drink from the water of Zamzam

6. Perform (7) cycles and walk between Safaa and Marwa

7. To complete your Umrah, you'll need to cut or trim your hair with some scissors. You can then go back to wearing normal clothes and hopefully behaving better than before.

Umrah can be done anytime throughout the year. Performing Umrah only requires you to stay in Makkah, while the rituals of Hajj will require you to do more and travel to other cities. For those who will perform Hajj must first perform Umrah and then proceed to perform the rituals of Hajj. When delivering a speech about Umrah, one must be very careful of what to say and what not to say. We pray to Allah (swt) to guide the speakers to give good talks about Umrah. Ameen!

II. Umrah Performance

Dear Brothers and Sisters: Assalamu `Alaikum

Thank you for inviting me to speak to you about how to perform Umrah. If you intend to perform Umrah and you are travelling from a far distance away from Makkah, such as USA, then please take not to the following:

Be thankful and grateful to Allah (swt) that He has inspired you to perform Umrah. This means that you'll go when it's not the Hajj (Pilgrimage) season. Therefore, the following rules will apply:

1. You should make the intention to perform Umrah

2. You must take a shower, pray 2 Rak'ah, and say Takbeer Labbaika

3. Before arriving to Jeddah put on Ihram clothes: Put on 2 pieces of cloth (like towels for men) and pray two Rak'ah

4. Keep yourself busy with the remembrance of Allah (swt) through (Zikr). Read Qur'an and make Du`aa' until you reach Makkah.

5. When you enter the Masjid of Ka'bah, make Tawaf around the Ka'bah, counter clockwise 7 times. Start from the corner of the Blackstone, circle 7 times and end there.

6. After you finish the Tawaf, make two Rak'ah Salat, and then drink from the water of Zamzam.

7. Then go to Safa and Marwa and make Sa'iy seven times.

8. Once you finish the Sa'iy, trim your hair and the Umrah ritual is over.

9. You can wear your normal clothing, and live a normal life.

III. Final Remarks

Dear Muslims

Allah (swt) is so generous to us. He gives us so many credits and blessings and for so many occasions. For those who go to Madina, the city of the Prophet (pbuh) and pray in his Masjid, Allah (swt) will give you 50,000 credits and blessings. For those who pray in Masjid Qubaa', located in the suburbs of Madina, Allah (swt) will give you blessings equal to that of Umrah. Moreover, whoever makes Umrah in the month of Ramadan will receive blessings equal to that of having made pilgrimage with our beloved Prophet Muhammad (pbuh).

Therefore, we encourage all Muslims to try to perform Umrah and Hajj as soon as possible, and as young as possible. We pray to Allah (swt) to bless all of us. Ameen!

Ka'bah in Makkah

I. Introduction

Dear Muslims

Assalamu `Alaikum

There are two types of Arafa; one is Arafa of Hajj and the other is Arafa of the Day of Judgment. The first Arafa takes place on Hajj (Pilgrimage) in the vicinity of Makkah. Muslims are required to perform Hajj at least once in their lifetime. Arafa is for one day only, it takes place once a year, and it is the 9th Day of the month of Zul-Hijjah. For that day, people live in tents as refugees. They must pray and ask Allah (swt) for forgiveness. That Day is known as the Day of Universal Forgiveness from Allah (swt), the Creator, to all those who ask for forgiveness.

The second Arafa is that of the Day of Judgment. This Arafa, the one of the Hereafter, is also One Day. Every person that ever lived will rise from their grave on the Day of Judgment. The sun will rise on that one day and will not set down until everyone is judged with fairness and justice by Allah (swt). The duration of that Day is at least a minimum of 1000 years according to our calculation. Allah (swt) says the following in Surah Al-Hajj (The Pilgrimage):

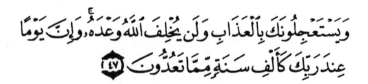

Yet they ask you to hasten on the Punishment! But Allah will not fail In His promise. Verily a Day in the sight of your Lord Is like a thousand years Of your reckoning. (22:47)

II. What Goes On

Dear Muslims

It should be stated here that the day of Arafa of the Hereafter is very awful and scary event that will take place on the Day of Judgment. It will be a very hard day for those who did wrong. The following list summarizes the sequence of events that will take place on that Day:

A. Angel Israfeel will be instructed by Allah (swt) to blow his trumpet twice. The first blow will cause the whole planet earth to shake and everything will cease to exist. The second blow will take place and water will be pored over. At that time, people will germinate and come out of their graves in a state of shock. Read Surah Al-Zumar (39:68).

B. After the trumpet has been blown by Angel Israfeel and the people are ready to come out of their graves, Allah (swt) instructs the earth to shake. While the quake is going on, people start coming out of their graves in a terrible state of shock. Allah (swt) has already informed the people in advance about this occasion. For more details, one may read Surah Al-Zalzalah (The Earthquake) (99:1-8).

C. People at that time will rise out of the grave with no clothes on or shoes. Those who are clothed will be very fortunate.

D. People will come out from their graves like scattered moths wondering where to go and what to do. They will be scared, baffled, and perplexed. For more details, one may read Surah Al-Qari`ah (the Great Calamity) (101:4)

E. When people rise from their graves, they will not believe what they are seeing. They will lose their mental concentration and start going in different directions without knowing where they are going. They will swarm like scattered locusts panicking in every direction, hoping to find a safe place until they lose all hope. For more details, one may refer to Surah Al-Qamar (The Moon) (54:7-8).

F. Currently, the sun is a distance of 92,870,000 miles above our heads and away from the earth. On that day of Arafa, the sun will sit only one mile above our heads.

G. The Arafa of the Hereafter will be so scary that nobody will be able to be concerned with or care for another; not even a mother for her child. People will be running away from each other even from their own beloved family members. For more details, refer to Surah Abasa (He Frowned) (80:33-37).

H. The more you read the Qur'an, the more you'll find serious and pertinent information regarding Arafa of the Day of Judgment. For more information, you may refer to Surah Al-Hajj (Pilgrimage) (22:1-2).

I. Many people would rather not know or be told about Arafa of the Day of Judgment. They would rather stay pre-occupied with the affairs of this world. And those who do know about the day of Arafa would rather forget as much as possible about the awfulness of that Day. They also would rather enjoy life on this planet earth without having to give much thought to what's going to happen on that Day. However, at some point, we are going to have to face the reality of Arafa of the Day of Judgment. On that day, people will wake up from their sleep and realize and remember all that they did in this world and what they'll have to account for with Allah (swt). For more information, one may refer to Surah Al-Naazi`aat (Those Who Tear Out) (79:34-41).

III. Final Remarks

Dear Muslims

Since the Day of Arafa of the Hereafter is going to be a hard test for us to get through, we should prepare ourselves in advance for that Day. We should repent and promise Allah (swt) to obey Him and to follow His Rules and Regulations before we visit the grave and it is too late. We should purify our intentions with Allah (swt) and start offering our good deeds and services to Him for the benefit of all mankind.

Further, you should try to perform Hajj (Pilgrimage) as soon as possible. By doing so, you'll have a chance to travel to Arafa, which is a city in the suburbs of Makkah, and you'll be able to comprehend the difficulty of making such a trip to the Arafa of Makkah. This trip should make you reflect on the trip you'll be taking to the Arafa of the Hereafter and how much more difficult that trip will be as compared to the trip to Arafa of Makkah. Accordingly, you'll feel sorry for yourself and you will want to repent and obey Allah (swt). Time passes very fast!! People should not delay their decision to go for Hajj. You don't know how long you have to live. I may not live to finish writing the last line of this book. Allahu A'lam- only Allah (swt) knows our date of departure from this world.

We hope and pray that people will take this topic seriously before it is too late. After death, there is no return back to this life. There is no repentance at the moment of death or after death.

Those who are smart and clever will take this advice seriously. They will plan for their Hereafter and they'll try to invest in their future eternal life. Let us pray for the best for everyone in this life and in the next life. Ameen!

Chapter (23)   New Hijra Year

I. Introduction

Dear Muslims

Assalamu `Alaikum

The Gregorian New Year marks the beginning of January. In as much as there is a Gregorian New Year, The Islamic New Year starts with the beginning of the month of Muharram.

The First Hijra year started at the time when Prophet Muhammad (pbuh) migrated from Makkah to Madinah in the Arabian Peninsula. It took place in the year of 622 C.E. Many Muslims all over the world celebrate the Islamic New Year. Their celebrations take place in the evening at the local mosques. They give lectures and offer other spiritual activities until about midnight, more or less. The government officials request that the religious scholars speak about this occasion on the local Radio and TV stations in order to inform, educate, and inspire the people about the relevance of the Migration, and its impact on the Muslims historically as well as today. The migration was a heroic achievement for the Prophet Muhammad (pbuh) as well as for our Ummah at large.

II. Migration Lesson

Dear Muslims

It should be stated here that anytime Muslims talk about the Islamic New Year, they are reminded of the Prophet's (pbuh) migration to Medina. A series of lessons can be learned from this:

1. They should migrate to another country seeking freedom of religion, freedom of speech, and better business opportunities.

2. They should migrate to seek political Asylum so that they are free from torture and persecution.

3. They should migrate for trade and business opportunities.

4. They should travel across the globe to be well informed and well educated about people in different parts of the world.

III. Life in Medina

Prophet Muhammad (pbuh) left Makkah to go live in Medina in order to escape persecution and be able to practice the True Religion of God (Islam) with his followers. He established a place of worship and lived next door to the mosque. He helped people the people of Medina to live together with the people of Makkah in peace and harmony irrespective of their color, nationality, religion, creed, ethnic background, positions, titles, or language.

IV. Final Remarks

Muslims around world generally are given the day off from school or work for the Islamic New Year. In U.S.A., it is recommended that the Islamic schools give the children the day off from school on that day. The school administrations should make sure to educate the students, staff, and teachers about the importance of the Prophet's (pbuh) migration (Hijra) and the impact of its achievement on the Muslim world.

We Muslims should study the Prophet's (pbuh) life history (Seerah) both when he lived in Makkah and after he migrated to Medina. He lived in Makkah for 13 years and in Medina for 10 years. In Medina, he was able to establish a society built on justice, fairness, and equality. He invited non-Muslims to accept Islam. Muslims in America should take a lesson from this and learn how to live united as immigrants with the indigenous Muslims in this country. We pray to Allah (swt) to guide us to the Sirat Mustaqeen. Ameen!

Chapter (24) Muharram / `Ashura

I. Introduction

Dear Muslims

Assalamu `Alaikum

Muharram is the first month of the lunar calendar year. It is one of the four (4) sacred months in Islam. Among the four are Zul Qi'dah (11th month); Zul Hijjah (12th month); Muharram (1st month); and Rajab (7th month).

Regarding the four sacred months, Allah (swt) says in the Qur'an in Surah Al-Tawbah (The Repentance) the following:

$$إِنَّ عِدَّةَ ٱلشُّهُورِ عِندَ ٱللَّهِ ٱثْنَا عَشَرَ$$
$$شَهْرًا فِى كِتَـٰبِ ٱللَّهِ يَوْمَ خَلَقَ ٱلسَّمَـٰوَٰتِ وَٱلْأَرْضَ$$
$$مِنْهَآ أَرْبَعَةٌ حُرُمٌ ذَٰلِكَ ٱلدِّينُ ٱلْقَيِّمُ فَلَا تَظْلِمُوا فِيهِنَّ$$
$$أَنفُسَكُمْ وَقَـٰتِلُوا ٱلْمُشْرِكِينَ كَآفَّةً كَمَا$$
$$يُقَـٰتِلُونَكُمْ كَآفَّةً وَٱعْلَمُوٓا أَنَّ ٱللَّهَ مَعَ ٱلْمُتَّقِينَ ۝$$

The number of months in the sight of Allah is twelve (in a year) - so ordained by Him the day He created the Heavens and the earth; Of them four are sacred; That is the Straight Religion..." (9:36)

The 10th day of the month of Muharram is called 'Ashura. It is a very significant day for the People of the Book, the Muslims, the early Christians, and the Jews. Allah (swt) saved the Jews in Egypt from Pharaoh with the help of Prophet Moses. This is also known as Exodus. Prophet Muhammad (pbuh) used to fast on the day of 'Ashura because Prophet Moses used to fast on that day and the Prophet (pbuh) considered Moses to be an older spiritual brother to him. Muslims are recommended to fast that day plus one other day. The reward from Allah (swt) is forgiveness for one whole year. The following Hadith is narrated by Abu Qitadah (May Allah be pleased with him) that the Prophet (pbuh) said:

عَـنْ أَبِي قَتَادَةَ رَضِيَ اللهُ عَنْهُ اَنَّ النبِيَّ صَلَّى اللهُ عَلَيهِ وَسَلَمٌ قَال :

«صَوْمُ يَوْمِ عَرَفَهَ يُكَفِّرُ سَنَتَيْنِ ، مَاضِيَةً وَمُسْتَقْبَلَةً، وَصَوْمُ يَوْمِ عَاشُورَاءَ يُكَفِّرُ سَنَةً مَاضِيَةً.»

— رواه الجماعة —

The fasting the day of Arafa gives forgiveness of two years. One year past and one year to come, and fasting the day of 'Ashura gives forgiveness of one past year.

II.   Significance

Dear Muslims

As for the importance of the month of Muharram and especially the Day of 'Ashura, the following are some Ahadith regarding their significance.

عَـنْ إِبْـنِ عَبّاسٍ رَضِيَ اللهُ عَنْهُما ،قَالَ : قَدِمُ النَّبِيُّ صَلَّى اللهُ عَلَيهِ وَسَلَّم المَدِينَةَ فَرَأى اليَهُودَ تَصُومُ عَاشُورَاءَ. فَقَالَ مَاهَذا؟ قَالُوا: يَوْمٌ صَالِحٌ. نَجَّى اللهُ فِيهِ مُوسَى وَبَنِي إِسْرَائِـيْـلَ مِـنْ عَدُوِّهِمْ، فَصَامَهُ مُوسَى. فَقَالَ النَّبِيُّ صَلَّى اللهُ عَلَيهِ وَسَلَّم : «أَنَا أَحَقُّ بِمُوسَى مِنكمْ.» فَصَامَهُ وَأَمَرَ بِصِيَامِهِ.

— متفق عليه —

83

Reported by Ibn Abbas (may Allah be pleased with them), saying that when the Prophet (pbuh) came to Medina, he found the Jews were fasting the day of 'Ashura. He asked about it. He was informed that it was a Good Day, where Allah saved Moses and the Children of Israel from their enemy. Hence, Moses fasted that Day. The Prophet (pbuh) said: I have more right unto Moses than you: He then fasted that day, and he ordered (them) to fast it.

During the Jahiliya period, before the advent of Islam, the Arabs used to respect that day and to fast it. It was reported:

عَنْ عَائِشَةَ رَضِيَ اللهُ عَنْهَا ، قَالَتْ :

« كَانَ يَوْمُ عَاشُورَاءَ يَوْماً تَصُومُهُ قُرَيْشٌ فِي الْجَاهِلِيَّةِ . وَكَانَ رَسُولُ اللهِ صَلَّى اللهُ عَلَيْهِ وَسَلَّمَ يَصُومُهُ . فَلَمَّا قَدِمَ الْمَدِينَةَ صَامَهُ وَأَمَرَ النَّاسَ بِصِيَامِهِ. فَلَمَّا فُرِضَ رَمَضَانُ ، قَالَ : مَنْ شَاءَ صَامَهُ وَمَنْ شَاءَ تَرَكَهُ »

ـ متفق عليه ـ

Narrated by Aisha (may Allah be pleased with her) saying: During the day of 'Ashura, the Quraish (tribe) used to fast it in the Jahiliya period. The Messenger of Allah used to fast it. When he came to Medina, he fasted it. When the month of Ramadan was prescribed as a fasting month, he said: Whoever wishes, let him fast it, ('Ashura) and whoever wishes let him not.

III. Generosity

Dear Muslims

Muslims are taught to be generous during the Day of 'Ashura. The following Hadith teaches the Muslims to be generous.

عَنْ جَابِرِ بْنِ عَبْدِ اللهِ رَضِيَ اللهُ عَنْهُ ، أَنَّ رَسُولَ اللهِ صَلَّى اللهُ
عَلَيْهِ وَسَلَّمَ قَالَ :
«مَنْ وَسَّعَ عَلَى نَفْسِهِ وَأَهْلِهِ يَوْمَ عَاشُورَاءَ ، وَسَّعَ اللهُ عَلَيْهِ سَائِرَ
سَنَتِهِ . »

*Reported by Jabir Ibn Abdullah® that the Prophet (pbuh)
said: Whoever is generous for himself and for his family the Day
of 'Ashura, Allah will be generous on him the rest of the year.*

The following Hadith is regards to the respect the Christians
and Jews had for the Day of 'Ashura:

عَنِ ابْنِ عَبَّاسٍ رَضِيَ اللهُ عَنْهُما ، قَالَ :
لَمَّا صَامَ رَسُولُ اللهِ صَلَّى اللهُ عَلَيْهِ وَسَلَّمَ يَوْمَ عَاشُورَاءَ وَأَمَرَ
بِصِيَامِهِ ، قَالُوا يَارَسُولَ اللهِ : إِنَّهُ يَوْمٌ تُعَظِّمُهُ الْيَهُودُ وَالنَّصَارَى ،
فَقَالَ : إِذَا كَانَ الْعَامُ الْمُقْبِلُ ــ إِنْ شَاءَ اللهُ ــ صُمْنَا الْيَوْمَ
التَّاسِعَ .

*Narrated by Ibn Abbas (may Allah be pleased with him)
saying: when the Messenger of Allah (pbuh) fasted the Day of
'Ashura, and commanded the Muslims to fast it, the Muslims said:
'O Messenger of Allah: it is a Day where Jews and Christians
respect it. He said: Next year (with the will of Allah) we will fast
the 9th day....'*

IV.   Final Remarks

Dear Muslims

On the other side of early history, Imam Hussein, grand child
of the Prophet Muhammad (pbuh), was coincidentally assassinated

on the same day of 'Ashura. Some groups of Muslims try to show their sorrows by commemorating this occasion of sadness in ways other than fasting.

We Muslims should study the Qur'an, Hadith and the Seerah of the Prophet Muhammad (pbuh). We should read more and more about our history from the correct sources so that we may know the significance of these historical events and know what Allah (swt) expects from us during these significant periods. We pray to Allah (swt) to bring peace and happiness to the world. The more Du`aa' (supplication) we make, the more Allah (swt) will send us peace and happiness all over the world. It is also important to dialogue with non-Muslims and inform them about Allah (swt). By doing so, Allah (swt) will take care of us. Ameen!

Glory and Praise are to Allah; Glory be to Allah The Most Great.

I. Introduction

Dear Muslims

Assalamu `Alaikum

My talk to you today is about <u>The Spirit of the New Year</u>. One year has elapsed in our life's history and another new year is coming upon us that we'll face. The doors of last year have been closed in our community however; the new year has opened new doors for its members.

The page of last year has turned and is now closed yet a new page has opened up for us in the New Year. The old page of last year closed with many memories, some miserable and some happy. However, the new, open page leaves us apprehensive about its content due to the unseen and unknown incidences, surprises and unpredictable news and information.

Dear Muslims

With the advent of every New Year, we should not follow nor act like the disbelievers by engaging ourselves in un-Islamic activities. On the eve of every new year, many people, particularly non-Muslims, have become accustomed to celebrating the advent of the new year by spending the whole night drinking, mingling and dancing. Unfortunately, some Muslims have followed in the footsteps of these unbelievers in this type of celebration.

II. Reflections

Dear Muslims

For a believing Muslim, the new year means more than just a passing incidence or occasion. It is an occasion for reflections. It is an occasion for us to think, ponder and act according to what Allah (swt) has prescribed for us in the Qur'an.

1. To reflect, to think and to ponder about the creation of Allah (swt) such as the sun and the moon through which the days, the weeks, the months and the years have been established in the solar and lunar systems. This is what Allah (swt) says in Surah Al-`Imran about pondering:

إِنَّ فِي خَلْقِ ٱلسَّمَـٰوَٰتِ وَٱلْأَرْضِ وَٱخْتِلَـٰفِ ٱلَّيْلِ وَٱلنَّهَارِ لَآيَـٰتٍ لِّأُوْلِي ٱلْأَلْبَـٰبِ ۞ ٱلَّذِينَ يَذْكُرُونَ ٱللَّهَ قِيَـٰمًا وَقُعُودًا وَعَلَىٰ جُنُوبِهِمْ وَيَتَفَكَّرُونَ فِي خَلْقِ ٱلسَّمَـٰوَٰتِ وَٱلْأَرْضِ رَبَّنَا مَا خَلَقْتَ هَـٰذَا بَـٰطِلًا سُبْحَـٰنَكَ فَقِنَا عَذَابَ ٱلنَّارِ ۞

Behold! In the creation of the heavens and the earth, and the alteration of Night and Day, there are indeed Signs for men of understanding - Men who remember Allah standing, sitting, and lying down on their sides and contemplate the (wonders of) creation in the heavens and the earth, (with saying): Our Lord not for naught have You created (all) this! Glory to You! Give us salvation from the Chastisement of the Fire. (3:190-191)

2. We should all reflect, think and ponder that one year of our life is over and that we are one year closer to death, one year closer to the end of our final life and one year closer to visiting the grave. A Muslim should remember death quite often so as to have pure actions and intentions in your daily life. Remember what Allah (swt) says in the Qur'an in Surah Al-Mulk (The Sovereignty):

88

تَبَـٰرَكَ ٱلَّذِى بِيَدِهِ ٱلْمُلْكُ وَهُوَ عَلَىٰ كُلِّ شَىْءٍ قَـدِيرٌ ١

ٱلَّذِى خَلَقَ ٱلْمَوْتَ وَٱلْحَيَوٰةَ لِيَبْلُوَكُمْ أَيُّكُمْ أَحْسَنُ عَمَلًا

وَهُوَ ٱلْعَزِيزُ ٱلْغَفُورُ ٢

Blessed be He in Whose hands is Dominion and He over all things has Power; He Who created death and life, that He may try which of which of you is best in deed; and He is the Exalted in Might; Oft-Forgiving. (67:1-2)

3. We should reflect, think and ponder about the condition of ourselves; physically, anatomically, biologically, pathologically, metabolically and the like. We should reflect, think and ponder about how each system functions, how each organ functions, how each tissue functions, how each atom functions and how each electron, neutron and proton functions. Finally, you should ask yourself, how do all these systems in our bodies coordinate their activities to systematically function all together, under normal and abnormal situations, so that we can live as normal human beings?

Dear Muslims

On the occasion of the new year, every Muslim should evaluate himself to see whether or not he has achieved his goals and objectives for the last year. You should ask what you have done for yourself, for your family, for your community, for the Muslim Ummah all over the world. A Muslim should question as to whether or not you performed the daily prayers regularly and on time. Did I fast the month of Ramadan with good intention? Did I read the Qur'an daily?

Did I help those who needed my help? Did I help others alleviate their problems? What was my role as a Muslim in this world? Did I fulfill my role as a Muslim in this world?

III. Final Remarks

Dear Muslims

May I request that you get together with your family members and hold a special session that will serve as a session of self-evaluation, self-criticism, self-analysis and self-study? After holding such a session, you and your family members should be able to come up with some resolutions, commitments and recommendations for the coming new year. When making these resolutions, remember that nothing can happen without the help of Allah (swt).

Dear Muslims

The occasion of the New Year should be a happy occasion. And in order for it to be so, may I kindly request that each and every one of you play your effective role in making this happiness a reality by acting accordingly and responsibly so that Allah (swt) may bless you and reward you. I ask Allah (swt) to forgive us for our shortcomings and reward us in the best way for what we have done. I ask Allah (swt) to help us purify our souls, our intentions and our motives. I ask Allah (swt) to help us to be the best examples and role models in society so that others may learn, imitate and follow us. I ask Allah (swt) to make the New Year a happy one for us and for all of Allah's (swt) creation. I ask Allah (swt) make us a source of happiness, a source of inspiration, a source of motivation, and a source of mobilization for others and to mankind. Ameen!

I. Introduction

Dear Muslims

Assalamu `Alaikum

The topic of my discussion is the Prophet's Birthday also known as Miladun Nabi. Prophet Muhammad (pbuh) was born on the 12th day of the month of Rabie' Al-Awwal. This is the 3rd lunar month in the Islamic calendar year. Many Muslim countries around the world celebrate this occasion publicly by having parades, speeches, lectures and government receptions. Others will invite the local Muslims to come to the Masjid and listen to the Imams, scholars and teachers speak about the personality and character of the Prophet (pbuh) and the Message he received from Allah (swt). Muslims usually take the day off from their jobs and their schools in order to participate in such an occasion.

Some Muslim countries may only resort to offering speeches and lectures on the radios and televisions, but they still consider it a big occasion. Very few countries consider this occasion an important one, but there is no need to do anything about it.

The Islamic schools here in the U.S.A do give the students a holiday break so the children can enjoy the celebration of the Prophet's Birthday. The wise Muslims do not really celebrate the birth of Prophet Muhammad (pbuh) but rather they try to commemorate the Seerah of his life during the month of Rabie' Al-Awwal.

It should be stated here that Muslims do believe in all the Prophets and Messengers of Allah (swt) that were sent to humanity since the creation of Adam and Eve. Allah (swt) has sent us about 124,000 prophets; however, in the Qur'an, Allah (swt) mentioned only twenty-five of them by name. Among the 25, He selected five (5) to be the most influential ones. They are Noah, Abraham,

Moses, Jesus and Muhammad (peace be upon them all).

In Professor Michael H. Hart's book, <u>The 100: A ranking of the Most Influential Persons in History</u>, he listed our beloved Prophet Muhammad (pbuh) as the number one most influential man in history. In his book, Michael Hart said, "My choice of Muhammad to lead the list of the world's most influential persons may surprise some readers and may be questioned by others, but he was the only man in history who was supremely successful on both the religious and secular levels".

Of humble origins, Muhammad (pbuh) founded and promulgated one of the world's great religions, and became an immensely effective political leader. Today, thirteen centuries after his death, his influence is still powerful and pervasive.

II. Speech

Dear Brothers/Sisters

Assalamu `Alaikum

We are thankful to Allah (swt) that we came here to commemorate the Seerah of Prophet Muhammad (pbuh). It is not enough to only celebrate his Birthday, rather we are here to commemorate and learn from the whole life of the Prophet. We should study his life and know that he was born an orphan, taken care of by his mother until she died, then taken care of by his grandfather until he died and then taken care of by his uncle Abu Talib and his wife Fatima until he grew up, married, and became a Prophet (pbuh).

We should know how he used to climb up to the Cave of Hiraa to contemplate, reflect and meditate there for all those years until he became a Prophet (pbuh). We should know about how difficult it was for him to deliver the Message of Allah (swt) to his relatives, his tribe, other Arab tribes, and finally the non-Muslims as well.

Dear Brothers/Sisters

We should remember all what Allah (swt) said about Prophet Muhammad (pbuh):

1. He is The Last Prophet (pbuh) and The Last Messenger of Allah (swt). In Surah Al-Ahzab (The Confederates), Allah (swt) says the following:

مَّا كَانَ مُحَمَّدٌ أَبَآ أَحَدٍ مِّن رِّجَالِكُمْ وَلَٰكِن رَّسُولَ ٱللَّهِ وَخَاتَمَ ٱلنَّبِيِّـۧنَ ۗ وَكَانَ ٱللَّهُ بِكُلِّ شَىْءٍ عَلِيمًا ﴿٤٠﴾

Muhammad is not the father of any of your men, but (he is) the Messenger of Allah, and the Seal of the Prophets: and Allah has full knowledge of all things. (33:40)

2. Prophet Muhammad (pbuh) has the Best manners and behavior. In the same Surah, Allah (swt) says the following:

لَّقَدْ كَانَ لَكُمْ فِى رَسُولِ ٱللَّهِ أُسْوَةٌ حَسَنَةٌ لِّمَن كَانَ يَرْجُواْ ٱللَّهَ وَٱلْيَوْمَ ٱلْأَخِرَ وَذَكَرَ ٱللَّهَ كَثِيرًا ﴿٢١﴾

You have indeed in the Messenger of Allah an excellent exemplar for him who hopes in Allah and the Final Day and who remember Allah much. (33:21)

3. Prophet Muhammad (pbuh) is the Best Example to follow and to mimic. In Surah Al-Qalam (The Pen), Allah (swt) says the following:

And surely you have sublime morals (68:4)

Dear Brothers and Sisters

Remember that the Prophet Muhammad (pbuh) is the summation, culmination and purification of all the previous Prophets and Messengers. Moreover, the Qur'an was revealed to the Prophet over a period of 23 years, (13) years in Makkah, and (10) years in Madinah. The Qur'an is a unique Book from Allah (swt) that was revealed in the Arabic language. It has been memorized by millions and millions of Muslims around the world, some who are Arab and many who are non-Arab. No single book has been memorized from cover to cover by more people than the Qur'an. It is really a happy revelation. As the Qur'an is being recited, one (Muslims and non-Muslims alike) cannot help but admire the beautiful rhythm and melody of the reciter's voice, which echoes in the hearts of the listeners and touches their souls.

Dear Brothers and Sisters

In attendance and observance of this noble occasion, I hope that we can study the Seerah of the Prophet (pbuh) and I hope that we can understand his teachings and apply them to our daily life. Further, we should try to teach and help others learn his teachings as well. Ameen!

I. Introduction

Many Muslims in different parts of the world observe the noble occasion of Israa' (night journey) and Mi'raaj (ascension to the heavens). This incident marks the calendar on the 27th day of Rajab in the Lunar Calendar of every year. This occasion has been mentioned in the Qur'an in two Surahs; once in Surah Al-Israa' (Night Trip) and the other in Surah Al-Najm (The Star). The Prophet (pbuh) was taken from Makkah to Jerusalem, followed by a journey to the upper heavens and back to his bed in Makkah all in one night.

II. Speech

Dear Muslims

Assalamu `Alaikum

We thank Allah (swt) for blessing us with His deen, Al-Islam. We thank all of you for joining us on this noble occasion of Israa' and Mi'raaj. I am sure you all came tonight to enjoy the spirituality of this occasion. I ask Allah (swt) to bless all of you and give you credit for leaving your houses and coming to the House of Allah (swt) for this event.

Dear Muslims

The story of Israa' and Mi'raaj took place after the Year of Sorrows. The Prophet (pbuh) lost his uncle Abu Talib and his beloved wife Khadija. He went to the city of Taa-if to deliver the Message of Allah (swt) but the people were so hostile towards him that they did not welcome his presence in their city. They were so cruel to him that they threw rocks at him until his legs were bleeding. He cried but he never cursed the people of Taa-if. Many of his companions had suffered cruel treatment as well.

Allah (swt) sent Angel Gabriel to take him for a Night Trip (Israa') from Makkah to Jerusalem to lead the Salat for all the previous prophets and messengers, about 125,000 of them, that ever lived before him. Then Angel Gabriel ascended with the Prophet (pbuh) to the upper heavens (Al-Mi'raaj) until they reached their Final Place in the upper heaven. Allah (swt) welcomed Prophet Muhammad (pbuh) and informed him about Salat. Allah (swt) wanted the Muslims to start praying 50 times a day. The Prophet Muhammad (pbuh) interceded on our behalf until Allah (swt) reduced the requirement to 5 times a day. Now we pray 5 times but we get credit of 50 prayers (10 credits for each prayer).

III. Final Remarks

Dear Muslims

Prayer was prescribed for us during the night of Israa' and Mi'raaj. By the Mercy of Allah (swt), we are only required to pray (5) daily Salat, as well as the Friday Salat. It is highly recommended that we pray Salat Taraweeh in Ramadan and the Salat of the two Eids. There is a special Salat that is done for a Funeral or Janazah. Furthermore, there are several other varieties of Salat, such as Salat Duha, Salat Wudoo', Salat Haajah, Salat Istikhara, Salat Tawba, Salat Tasbeeh, and so on and so forth.

Dear Muslims

Remember, Salat is a communication between you and Allah (swt). We pray, we read Qur'an, and we talk to Allah (swt), but Salat is like a Mi'raaj. It is a spiritual ascension from this world to the upper Heavens. Salat helps us to clean and purify ourselves. It permeates our bodies to help improve our condition spiritually, mentally, and physically. We ask Allah (swt) to accept our Salat and our Du'aa'. Allahumma Ameen!

I.   Introduction

Dear Muslims

Assalamu `Alaikum

As we mentioned before, Israa' & Mi'raaj took place during The Year of Sorrows. The Prophet (pbuh) lost his wife Khadija and then his uncle Abu Talib. He and his companions were trapped in the suburbs of Makkah for three years without being allowed to leave. When he went to the city of Al Taa-if to deliver the Message of Allah (swt), the local people sent the youth to throw rocks at him. As he was bleeding from his legs and in pain, he cried out to Allah (swt) and asked what should he do? Angel Gabriel descended upon him and asked the Prophet (pbuh) if he wants Allah (swt) to send a calamity (an earthquake) upon the people of Makkah and Taa-if for their mischievous behavior and bad deeds. The Prophet (pbuh) said, "NO"! He said that it's possible that their children may accept Islam and become Muslims.

II. Israa' Trip (The Night Journey)

Dear Muslims

Angel Gabriel came to the Prophet (pbuh) at night and took him from his bed in Makkah and took him on a night journey to Jerusalem. They made several stops on the way. Angel Gabriel stopped in Yathrib (Madina) where the Prophet (pbuh) prayed. He was then told this place will be the city of your migration. Then the Prophet (pbuh) was taken to Mt. Toor, where Moses received the Ten Commandments. Then he was taken to Bethlehem where Jesus was born. Finally he visited the Sacred Mosque in Jerusalem. There Prophet Muhammad (pbuh) led the prayer (Salat) for all the 125,000 previous prophets and messengers that came before him. They all prayed behind Prophet Muhammad (pbuh) as their Imam, their leader and a peace maker.

III. Mi'raaj

Dear Muslims

For Mi'raaj, the Prophet (pbuh) was taken from Jerusalem to the upper heavens to receive the instruction about the five (5) daily prayers. He was returned back to his bed in the same night. This trip took place on the 27th day of Rajab, which is the seventh lunar month. Muslims all over the world, specifically in the U.S.A., observe this Spiritual Night in many different mosques.

IV. What Qur'an says:

There are two chapters in the Qur'an where Israa' and Mi'raaj are mentioned. In Chapter 17, Surah is Al-Israa' (The Night Travel) Allah (swt) says the following:

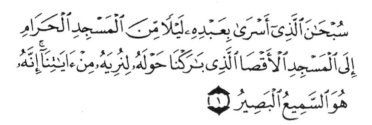

Glory to (Allah) Who did take His Servant for a Journey by night from the Sacred Mosque to the farthest Mosque whose precincts We did bless - In order that We might show him some of Our Signs: For He is the One Who hears and sees (all things). (17:1)

In Surah An-Najm (The Star), Allah (swt) tells us about his ascension from the **Dome of the Rock** Masjid to the upper heavens to receive the revelation about the daily prayers. The verses in that chapter are the following:

بِسْمِ اللَّهِ الرَّحْمَنِ الرَّحِيمِ

وَالنَّجْمِ إِذَا هَوَىٰ ١ مَا ضَلَّ صَاحِبُكُمْ وَمَا غَوَىٰ ٢ وَمَا يَنطِقُ
عَنِ الْهَوَىٰ ٣ إِنْ هُوَ إِلَّا وَحْىٌ يُوحَىٰ ٤ عَلَّمَهُ شَدِيدُ الْقُوَىٰ ٥
ذُو مِرَّةٍ فَاسْتَوَىٰ ٦ وَهُوَ بِالْأُفُقِ الْأَعْلَىٰ ٧ ثُمَّ دَنَا فَتَدَلَّىٰ ٨
فَكَانَ قَابَ قَوْسَيْنِ أَوْ أَدْنَىٰ ٩ فَأَوْحَىٰ إِلَىٰ عَبْدِهِ مَا أَوْحَىٰ ١٠
مَا كَذَبَ الْفُؤَادُ مَا رَأَىٰ ١١ أَفَتُمَارُونَهُ عَلَىٰ مَا يَرَىٰ ١٢ وَلَقَدْ رَآهُ
نَزْلَةً أُخْرَىٰ ١٣ عِندَ سِدْرَةِ الْمُنتَهَىٰ ١٤ عِندَهَا جَنَّةُ الْمَأْوَىٰ ١٥
إِذْ يَغْشَى السِّدْرَةَ مَا يَغْشَىٰ ١٦ مَا زَاغَ الْبَصَرُ وَمَا طَغَىٰ ١٧ لَقَدْ رَأَىٰ
مِنْ آيَاتِ رَبِّهِ الْكُبْرَىٰ ١٨

By the star when it goes down, Your Companion is neither astray nor being misled, nor does he say (aught) of (his own) desire. Is no less than inspiration sent down to him: He was taught by one Mighty in Power, endued with Wisdom: For he appeared (in stately form) while he was in the highest part of the horizon: Then he approached and came closer, and he was at a distance of but two bow-length or (even) nearer; So did (Allah) convey the inspiration to His servant-(conveyed) what He (meant) to convey. The (Prophet's (mind and) heart in no way falsified that which he saw. Will you then dispute with him concerning what he saw? For indeed he saw him at a second descent, near the Lote-tree of the utmost boundary. Near it is the garden of abode. Behold, the Lote- tree was shrouded with what shrouds.

(His) sight never swerved, nor did it go wrong! For truly did he see of the signs of his Lord, the Greatest! **(53:1-18)**

V. Final Remarks

The wisdom that we can benefit from this occasion is that a Muslim should pray five (5) times a day and should attend the Masjid on Fridays to join the congregation for the Khutbah and the Salat. There are a variety of different Salat that can be performed in Islam. Here is a list of some of them:

1. Salat of the two feast (Eids)
2. Salat Al-Haajah
3. Salat Al-Istighaarah
4. Salat Al-Khusoof and Kusoof
5. Salat Al-Tawbah
6. Salat Al-Tassbeeh
7. Salat Al-Taraweeh during Ramadan
8. Salat Al-Duhaa
9. Salat Al-Wudoo'
10. Salat Tahiyatul Masjid, etc. , etc.

We pray to Allah (swt) to bless the Muslims all over the world. May Allah (swt) keep us as Muslims who practice all the Pillars of Islam. Allahumma Ameen!

I. Introduction

Dear Muslims

Assalamu `Alaikum

The month of Sha'ban is the 8th month of the lunar calendar. The 15th day of Sha'ban is known as the night of Baraa-ah (forgiveness). Many Muslims in different parts of the world observe this special occasion by holding spiritual gatherings at night in the mosques. Since this day is a couple of weeks before Ramadan, some will prepare special sweets while others will have picnics in order for them to enjoy themselves before the fasting begins. Others will choose to fast in an attempt to get closer to Allah (swt) and to prepare themselves spiritually and physically to fast in the month of Ramadan. Some Muslims countries will observe this day by giving the local people the day off while other Muslim countries will no such vacation. The Prophet (pbuh) used to fast most of the month of Sha'ban and he used to stop fasting after the 15th day. He was asked about this month and the Prophet (pbuh) informed his companions about how important this month is in the Book of Allah (swt). In this month, the records of people's deeds are lifted up to Allah (swt) on a daily basis, and the Prophet (pbuh) stated that he wishes to be in a state of fasting.

II. Sayings of the Prophet (pbuh)

Dear Muslims

Here, I will report some sayings of the Prophet (pbuh) about the significance of this particular day and night. To be more specific, the following is a partial list of Hadith from the Prophet (pbuh) about fasting during the month of Sha'ban:

1. 'Aisha said: "I never saw the Messenger of Allah fast a complete month except for Ramadan, and I have never

seen him fast more in a month than he did in Sha'ban."
This is related by al-Bukhari and Muslim.

2. Usamah Ibn Zaid inquired, "O Messenger of Allah, I never find you fasting in any month like you do during the month of Sha'ban". The Prophet (pbuh) responded, "That is a month that people neglect. It comes between Rajab and Ramadan. It is a month in which the deeds are raised to the Lord of the Worlds. I love that my deeds be raised while I am fasting". This is related by Abu Dawud, an-Nasaa-ee and by Ibn Khuzaimah in his Sahih.

3. Mu'az Ibn Jabal® reported that the prophet (pbuh) said, "Allah (swt) looks toward all His creatures the night of the 15th of the month of Sha'ban, and He forgives all His creatures except a Mushrik (The one who associates someone with Allah), or a trouble maker".

4. Al-Baihaqee® reported that 'Aisha heard the Prophet (pbuh) saying, "Angel Gabriel came to me and said, this is the night of the 15th of Sha'ban; Allah (swt) is to free and to liberate people from Hell fire, their number is equal to the number of hair on lambs; Allah (swt) does not look at the Muskrik; not at the argumentative person; not at the one who broke relationship with his relatives; not at those who lower their clothes to the grounds; not at those who are disrespectful (undutiful, disobedient) to their parents, and not at those who are addicted to alcohol..., etc".

5. Ali®, the cousin of the Prophet (pbuh), reported that the Prophet (pbuh) said to the believers, "When the night of the 15th of Sha'ban is here, wake up that night and fast during the day". Allah (swt) comes down to this planet at the time of sunset and He asks, Is there anyone who asks

for forgiveness and I will forgive him? Is there anyone who is asking for sustenance and I will nourish him? Is there anyone who is being tested with sickness and I will give him good health? Is there any...any...any... till the time of dawn. (Ibn Majah Reported)

III. Final Remarks

Dear Muslims

Since you came tonight to learn more and to refresh your memories about this day, I ask Allah (swt) to bless you and reward you for your efforts. If you wish to pray extra Salat tonight, I encourage you to join us for the prayers we will make in jama'at (as a group). You will receive more credits and rewards from Allah (swt) by praying together. Since tomorrow is the 15th day of Sha'ban, I encourage you all to fast as the Prophet (pbuh) did on this day. It is your choice, between you and Allah (swt), and if you do, you will be blessed more and more Insha-Allah.

Dear Muslims

I also would like to encourage you to read the Qur'an and listen to its recitation on a daily basis. The month of Ramadan is quickly approaching so please try to prepare yourselves to welcome it in good spirits. Try to come to Masjid as often as you possibly can. Give as much charity (Sadaqa) to the poor and the needy people as possible. If possible, visit the cemetery and make special supplications (Du`aa') for all. May Allah (swt) bless you and reward you.

Before we leave tonight, let us read together Surah Yaseen, Surah Al-Waqi'ah and Surah Al-Mulk in addition to Ayah Kursi and the four Surahs that start with Qull. We pray for happiness. Ameen!

Chapter (30)   About Fasting (Part 1)

I.   Introduction

Dear Muslims

Assalamu `Alaikum

Fasting during the month of Ramadan is the fourth pillar of Islam. All Muslims are obligated to fast unless they are pardoned. There are rules and regulations that define how we should fast and what excuses us from the fast. Muslims fast as a sign of their obedience to Allah (swt), the Creator of the universe. In addition to receiving blessings and rewards from Allah (swt) for the fast, Muslims may benefit in other ways such as socially, economically, spiritually, culturally, psychologically, medically, and many more. There are many other types of fasting that was prescribed outside the teachings of Islam. The People of the Book (Christians and Jews) were ordained by Allah (swt) to show their obedience to Him by fasting in a different way.

We hope and pray that Allah (swt) will accept us and all our efforts and deeds that we do individually or collectively. We ask Allah (swt) to forgive our shortcomings. Allahumma Ameen!

II.   Levels of Fasting

Dear Muslims

Imam Ghazali, in his book of Ihyaa' 'Ulum Al-Din, informs us that there are three levels of Fasting:

1.   The fasting of the general public (`Umoom)
2.   The fasting of the select few   (Khusoos)
3.   The fasting of the elite among the select few (Khusoos Al-Khusoos)

III. Blessings of Fasting

Dear Muslims

The benefits of fasting in the month of Ramadan are too many to be counted. If anyone could recognize and/or realize its benefit or importance, they would wish every month to be the month of Ramadan throughout the whole year. Allah (swt) gives many blessings to the fasting Muslims who are fasting with full faith and expectation.

Some of Allah's (swt) blessings and benefits for fasting in the month of Ramadan are listed below and have been grouped and summarized into different categories. They are only listed here without commentary. The list of blessings was taken directly from the Qur'an and the Hadith. Please remember that this is only a partial list of blessings and benefits for fasting during Ramadan.

1. Taqwa
2. Protection from Shaitan
3. Forgiveness
4. Multiple Rewards
5. Blessings During Sahoor
6. Blessings of Taraweeh
7. Blessings of Lailatul Qadr
8. Zakat, Sadaqa, generosity and Blessings
9. Good Health
10. Umrah in Ramadan equals Hajj

IV. Final Remarks

Fasting the month of Ramadan is one of the five pillars of Islam. Fasting other days outside of this noble month is highly recommended. The whole idea of fasting is to seek Allah's (swt) pleasure and earn His blessings. In addition, the fasting of a

Muslim will bring many other benefits to their life. One of the most important benefits that a Muslim achieves from fasting is the Taqwa in the heart. The reference for fasting can be found directly in the Qu'ran, the divinely revealed scripture of Islam and delivered by the Prophet Muhammad (pbuh). Allah (swt) says in Surah Al-Baqarah (The Cow) the following:

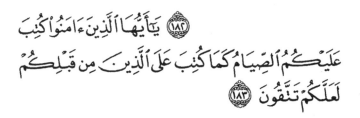

O you who believe! Fasting is prescribed to you as it was prescribed to those before you, that you may (learn) self-restraint. (2:183)

The Revelations in the Qur'an are considered to be a guide for all mankind. The Scrolls of Prophet Ibrahim were revealed to him in the month of Ramadan just as the Zaboor, Torah, and Injeel were revealed to Dawood, Moses, and Jesus respectively in the month of Ramadan. And just like the others, the Qur'an was also first revealed in the month of Ramadan. For this reason, Muslims fast to fulfill a very serious religious obligation that denotes the advent of Islam and the revelation of the Holy Qur'an. Muslims also believe that Ramadan confers great blessings.

We pray to Allah (swt) to grant us the strength, health, and patience so that we will continue to fast in the month of Ramadan and many other days throughout the year.

We ask Allah (swt) to continue to bless our Muslim Ummah with many blessings in the month of Ramadan. Ameen!

Chapter (31)　　About Fasting (Part 2)

I.　Introduction

Dear Muslims

Assalamu `Alaikum

As we said, Muslims fast in the month of Ramadan to fulfill a religious obligation in order to please Allah (swt) and to earn His blessings and rewards.

Fasting in the month of Ramadan is the fourth of the five pillars in Islam. The other four are Shahadah (the declaration of faith), Salat (5 daily prayers), Zakat (giving alms to the poor), and Hajj (performing pilgrimage to Makkah). Ramadan falls in the ninth month of the Islamic lunar calendar. Depending on the sighting of the moon, Ramadan begins eleven or twelve days earlier with each successive year.

II.　Significance of Fasting

Dear Muslims

People have many different reasons why they'll fast, depending upon the social, religious, and economic understanding of each individual person. Dr. Allan Cott, author of Fasting: The ultimate Diet, explains about some of the reasons why people choose to fast. Here's what he had to say in his book:

1. To lose weight the quickest and easiest way
2. To feel better physically and mentally
3. To look and feel younger
4. To save money
5. To give the whole system a rest
6. To cleanse out the body
7. To lower blood pressure and cholesterol levels
8. To cut down or quit smoking and drinking
9. To get more out of sex

10. To allow the body to heal itself
11. To relieve tension
12. To stop drug addictions
13. To sleep better
14. To improve food digestion
15. To regulate the bowels
16. To feel euphoric
17. To sharpen the senses
18. To quicken mental processing
19. To save time
20. To boost self-esteem
21. To learn better eating habits
22. To empathize and share with the hungry (less fortunate)
23. To gain or increase self control
24. To seek out spiritual revelations
25. To observe religious rites
26. To call attention to social issues and social justice
27. To slow the aging process

III. Types of Fasting

Dear Muslims

Although there are several types of fasting in Islam, all involve the same sequential pattern, obligations, rules and regulations, and food habits. The differences between them are in the number of days one will fast and whether or not the fast is mandatory, supererogatory, or optional.

The type of fasting that is prescribed in Islam is considered to be a complete and total type of fasting. Muslims abstain from food, drink, and matrimonial relations from the time of dawn until the time the sun sets. After the sun goes down, the Muslims may resume their eating, drinking and matrimonial relationships.

The types of Islamic fasting can be summarized as follows:

1. Mandatory
2. Supererogatory Fasting
3. Recommended Fasting
4. Forbidden Fasting
5. Fasting for Atonement

IV. Final Remarks

Dear Muslims

Fasting in the month of Ramadan has been prescribed and revealed by Allah (swt) to all human beings; for them to benefit from in this world and in the Hereafter. We Muslims should try to keep ourselves attached to seeking the pleasure of Allah (swt) daily. The reward of Fasting is forgiveness. We are encouraged to also fast voluntarily intermittently on Mondays and Thursdays through out the entire year and as much as possible during the months of Rajab, Shawwal, Sha'ban, Zul-Qidah, Zul Hijjah, and Muharram.

We ask Allah (swt) to inspire us all to keep in touch with Him and stay close to Him as long as we are alive. Ameen!

There is no deity except Allah
Muhammad is the Messenger of Allah

I. Introduction

Dear Muslims

Assalamu `Alaikum

Lailatul Qadr is known as the Night of Power. It falls on an odd night within the last ten days in the month of Ramadan. It could specifically be the night of the 27th day of Ramadan or can fall on any of the other odd nights, i.e. 21, 23, 25, or 29. The Qur'an was revealed on that night as a guide to mankind. This night, Lailatul Qadr, is more important than one thousand months.

Allah (swt) revealed and named one of the chapters in the Qur'an after Lailatul Qadr. In Surah Al-Qadr (The Night of Power.), the revelation reads as follows:

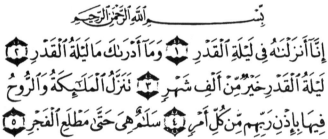

We have indeed revealed this (message) in the Night of Power. And what will explain to you what the Night of Power is? The Night of Power is better than a thousand months. Therein come down the angels and the Spirit by Allah's permission, on every errand: Peace! This until the rise of Morn. (97:1-5)

There is another chapter in the Qur'an reaffirming the Revelation of Qur'an during the Night of Power. That chapter is called Ad-Dukhaan (Smoke or Mist). The following 6 Ayahs are revealed in this Surah of the Qur'an:

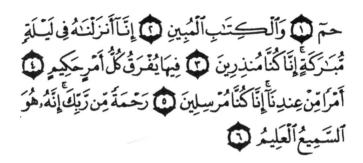

Ha Meem. By the Book that makes things clear; - We sent it down during a blessed night for We (ever) wish to warn (against Evil). In that (night) is made distinct every affair of wisdom, by command, from Us. For We (ever) send (revelations), as a Mercy from your Lord; for He hears and knows (All things). (44:1-6)

II. Celebration

Muslims, all over the world, observe and commemorate Lailatul Qadr by spending the night at the Masajid in order to pray, worship and cherish the spirituality of this great night of power. This night takes place about three (3) days before the Feast of Eid-ul-Fitr. In the Muslim world, people do not go to work or school from that night until the celebration of Eid-ul-Fitr is over. The Islamic schools in the US give the children the day off from school as well. However, the public schools in America don't have the same allowances so it is recommended that the Muslim students that are enrolled in public schools be excused from school the day after Lailatul Qadr and not to be penalized for it. The same goes for the parents, we recommend they take one day off from work so that they too can enjoy the Spiritual Night of Lailatul Qadr.

During the last ten days of the month of Ramadan, many Muslims perform what is called I'tikaf (Spiritual Retreat). Some

111

of the members of the community live in the Masjid for the last ten days of Ramadan and isolate themselves from the rest of the world in order to focus on their worship to Allah (swt). In the Masjid, they spend their time on prayer, meditation, reading Qur'an, and making du`aa' to Allah (swt). Muslims do this out of love and devotion to Allah (swt), to elevate their status with Allah (swt), and to follow the Prophet's (pbuh) Sunnah. If an employee wishes to take time off from work to do I'tikaf, their request should be granted, especially if it is part of their yearly vacation time.

III. Final Remarks

Dear Respected Muslims

The night of Power is so mighty in the sight of Allah (swt) that He describes it in the Qur'an as being better than one thousand months or 83.3 years of our life. My recommendation to each and everyone one of you is to encourage every Muslim to observe this Night with as much devotion to Allah (swt) as possible. We ask Allah (swt) to inspire all of us to pray, read Qur'an, listen to its recitation, go to the Masjid, and make Du`aa' (supplication) daily.

Dear Muslims

I am sure every one of us would like to live a life free of sins and free of mistakes. And I am sure you all would like to meet Allah (swt) on the Day of Judgment with a clear record, feeling free and happy as a newborn. Wouldn't you like to rejuvenate yourself and start a new year with a fresh new outlook? Don't you want to purify yourself and be without anguish or torment in order to live a pure life? The **Night of Power** is one of the best ways in which a person can achieve all these benefits. For this reason, I'd like to suggest that you start looking for Lailatul Qadr so that you'll be able to observe it and enjoy its blessings. Allahumma Ameen!

I. Introduction

Dear Muslims

Assalamu `Alaikum

My talk to you today is about Lailatul Qadr, The Night of Power. This was a very important occasion in the history of Islam and has a significant impact on our personal lives. In the previous speech, I mentioned twice the importance of this occasion. We should remind ourselves about its significance to the Revelation of Qur'an. In Surah Al-Baqarah (The Cow), Allah (swt) says the following:

شَهْرُ ﴿١٨٤﴾ رَمَضَانَ ٱلَّذِىٓ أُنزِلَ فِيهِ ٱلۡقُرۡءَانُ هُدًى لِّلنَّاسِ وَبَيِّنَٰتٍ مِّنَ ٱلۡهُدَىٰ وَٱلۡفُرۡقَانِ فَمَن شَهِدَ مِنكُمُ ٱلشَّهۡرَ فَلۡيَصُمۡهُ وَمَن كَانَ مَرِيضًا أَوۡ عَلَىٰ سَفَرٍ فَعِدَّةٌ مِّنۡ أَيَّامٍ أُخَرَ يُرِيدُ ٱللَّهُ بِكُمُ ٱلۡيُسۡرَ وَلَا يُرِيدُ بِكُمُ ٱلۡعُسۡرَ وَلِتُكۡمِلُوا ٱلۡعِدَّةَ وَلِتُكَبِّرُوا ٱللَّهَ عَلَىٰ مَا هَدَىٰكُمۡ وَلَعَلَّكُمۡ تَشۡكُرُونَ ﴿١٨٥﴾

Ramadan is the (month) in which was sent down the Qur'an, as a guide to mankind, also clear (Signs) for guidance and judgment (between right and wrong). So every one of you who is present (at his home) during that month should spend it in fasting, but if anyone is ill, or on a journey, the prescribed period (should be made up) by days later. Allah intends every facility for you;

113

He does not want to put you to difficulties. (He wants you) to complete the prescribed period, and to glorify Him in that He has guided you; and perchance you shall be grateful. (2:185)

II. Prophet's saying:

A. Prophet Muhammad (pbuh) said about Lailatul-Qadr:

عن أبي هريرة أن النبي صلى الله عليه وسلم قال : " مَن قام ليلة القَدر إيماناً واحتساباً غُفِرَ له ما تقدم من ذنبه "

ـ رواه البخاري ومسلم ـ

It was narrated by Abu Hurairah that the Prophet (pbuh) said: *Anyone who stays awake for the Night of Power with belief and for the pleasure of Allah (swt), all his previous sins will be forgiven.*

Reported by Bukhari and Muslim

B. It has also been reported by `Aisha, the wife of the Prophet (pbuh) who said:

عن عائشة رضي الله عنها قالت : قلت يا رسول الله أرأيت إن علمت أيّ ليلة ليلة القدر ما أقول فيها ؟ قال : قولي : اللهُمَّ إنك عَفوٌ تحب العَفو فأعفُ عنّي "

I asked the Messenger of Allah (pbuh), "if I knew which night was the Night of Power what prayer should I say during that night?" He said to me, Say: *"O Allah! You are forgiving and You love forgiveness, so You too forgive me."*

114

III. Signs of Lailatul Qadr

Dear Muslims

Although we do not know exactly which night Lailatul Qadr, Night of Power, will fall on but we do know that it has been reported to be one of the odd numbered nights of the last ten days of Ramadan, i.e. 21st, 23rd, 25th, 27th or 29th. It has been emphasized that it is most likely to fall on the 27th night but only Allah (swt) has true knowledge of what night it is.

The following is a list of physical signs that will help us to identify Lailatul Qadr:
1. The sun rises early in the morning without rays.
2. Rain may fall either during the night or next day.
3. During the night the sky will be slightly foggy.
4. The sky will be slightly lighted without reflections and without rays.
5. The angles, including Gabriel will descend down to earth for many purposes.

IV. Final Remarks

Dear Muslims

In summary, I would like to mention the following:

The Night of Power is a very important occasion for Muslims. Every one is encouraged to seek and strive to observe this extraordinary night. Lailatul Qadr is a night of Mercy, a night of Blessing, a night of Peace and a night of Guidance. It is a night of unification between the finite world we live in and the infinite universe of the unseen.

Anyone who is seeking to attain the Mercy of Allah (swt) will strive very hard to look for the Night of Power. Anyone who would like to share in the blessings of Allah (swt) on this blessed Night will strive to know and identify the Night of Power. Anyone who is interested in attaining peace of mind, peace of body and peace in society must look for Lailatul Qadr and worship in it.

May Allah (swt) give us the strength, the power, the courage and the conviction to do our best, obey Him, and follow His teachings. May Allah (swt) guide us and may He (swt) strengthen our Iman. May Allah (swt) help us to live another year with sincerity and devotion to Him. May Allah (swt) make us realize that one year of our life is over and we are one year closer to visiting our grave.

Let us wake up with a renewed intention to do our best to please Allah (swt) in our daily life. Let us also ask Almighty Allah (swt) for forgiveness. Ameen!

To those who do good there is good in this world
And the Home of the Hereafter is even better
and excellent indeed is the Home of the righteous.

I.   Introduction

Dear Muslims

Assalamu `Alaikum

The title of my talk is about Du`aa' (Supplication) to Allah (swt). This topic is a unique one indeed. Allah (swt) says in the Qur'an in Surah Al-Ghafir (The Forgiver), the following:

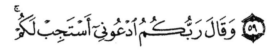

And Lord says: Call on Me; I will answer your supplication (Du`aa'). (40:60)

Allah (swt) is asking and commanding people to call upon Him so that He may answer their calls and their Du`aa'.  The word Du`aa' has been mentioned in the Qur'an at least two hundred and six (206) times. As one can see, this subject is very important in Islam and for this reason it is better to discuss it in summary.

Dear Muslims

Sometimes as humans, we feel a pressing need to call someone for help in order to get a troubling issue resolved. In these times, we should feel desperate to call upon Allah (swt) for His Help, His Support, His Guidance, His Mercy and His Forgiveness. For this reason, we should turn to Allah (swt) any time we need Him. We don't need any special communication equipment to talk with Him but we do need to fulfill some special prerequisites before we make the call. There is no need to go to a special building nor do we need to use a special operator, special booth, or special agent to make the call. There is no special time to call upon Him as He is ready to hear our call twenty four hours a day throughout the whole year. The frequency and the duration of the calls are important in the sense that the more you call upon Allah (swt) the more He will be happy with you. Moreover, the longer you are in a state of calling upon Him, the better the outcome will be for you.

II. Prerequisites

Dear Muslims

This type of calling upon Allah (swt) is a wireless system of communication. It is private entity and is very fast. It is a coded system, which is composed of six codes. Each code corresponds to a state of action, a state of practice or a state of application. In order for the Du`aa' to be answered by Allah (swt), two major factors must take place; two **Prerequisites** must be fulfilled and four **Requirements** must also be fulfilled. The two prerequisites are outlined in Surah Al-Baqarah (The Cow) as follows:

وَإِذَا سَأَلَكَ عِبَادِى عَنِّى فَإِنِّى قَرِيبٌ أُجِيبُ دَعْوَةَ ٱلدَّاعِ إِذَا دَعَانِ ۖ فَلْيَسْتَجِيبُواْ لِى وَلْيُؤْمِنُواْ بِى لَعَلَّهُمْ يَرْشُدُونَ ﴿١٨٦﴾

When My servants ask you concerning Me, I am indeed (close to them): I respond to the prayer of every suppliant when he calls on Me: let them also, with a will, listen to My call, and believe in Me: that they may walk in the right way. (2:186)

Therefore, the prerequisites are:

1. One must have deep faith (Iman) in Allah (swt) and His Messenger Muhammad (pbuh).
2. One must accept all of Allah's (swt) rules and regulations in our daily life activities (Istijabah).

118

These two prerequisites are very much needed if any person wishes to call upon Allah (swt). On the other hand, if we only claim that we believe in Allah (swt) but we do not follow His orders properly and we do not practice His teachings correctly then the response to our Du`aa' will be nil.

Dear Muslims

We must realize that these prerequisites do not guarantee the answer to our calls but they do assure us that we have aligned ourselves onto the right path. This leaves us to search and find out what the remaining requirements are in order for us to ensure a positive answer from Allah (swt). We also need to remind ourselves of what Allah (swt) said concerning the previous two requirements; Allah (swt) said, **that they may get the mercy and guidance of Allah (swt).** Also, they may get the answer to their call from Allah (swt).

III. Requirements

How we ask Allah (swt), how we call upon Him, the tone we use to talk to Him, the feelings we have in His presence, the posture we carry in His presence, the pitch of our voice, the attitude we have and the many other factors are among the requirements that will affect a positive answer from Allah (swt). Please read what Allah (swt) says in the Qur'an in Surah Al-A'raf (The Heights). (7:55-56)

This means that there are four requirements to be followed so that the Du`aa' will be accepted by Allah. These factors are:

1. **Tadarru'**		تضــرع
2. **Khufiyah**		خفيـــة
3. **Khawf**		خــوف
4. **Tama'**		طمــع

IV. Final Remarks

Dear Muslims

The Qur'an is full of Du`aa'. It is recommended that each one of us should get a copy of the Qur'an and read it so that we can learn the verses that are related to Du`aa'. The Qur'an is really the best source for learning about the Du`aa' that is accepted by Allah (swt). If we say them in our daily life, we will be rewarded by Allah (swt) indeed. Therefore, may I request you kindly read the Qur'an daily and learn the Du`aa' from it, and then make these Du`aa' regularly. Remember what Prophet Muhammad (pbuh) said,

» الدُّعَاءُ مُخُّ العِبَادَةِ «

"Supplication is the brain of worship."

Let us increase our call to Allah (swt) and let us have the utmost respect for Allah (swt) when we call upon Him. Let us request from Almighty Allah (swt) to grant us guidance, forgiveness and mercy. Ameen!

There is No Deity except Allah,
And Muhammad is the
Messenger Of Allah.

Chapter (35)   Supplications (Du`aa')   (Part 2)

I.   Introduction

Dear Muslims

Assalamu `Alaikum

Du`aa' is something that is done between you and the Creator, namely Allah (swt). We need Him; however, He does not need us because He created us and chose us to represent Him on this planet earth. He also subjugated so many things in the universe for our benefits. As human beings, we are liable to make mistakes. Therefore, we should apologize to Allah (swt), ask for forgiveness, and promise not to repeat our mistakes with ill intentions. In order to erase our mistakes, we must take the initiative to replace our mistakes by performing good deeds. By doing this, you'll replace the bad deed with credits and blessings from Allah (swt). Ameen!

II.   Who's Du`aa' is Accepted

The following is a partial list of groups of people whose Du`aa' has been assured to be accepted by Allah (swt):

1. The Desperate
2. Those where injustice was inflicted upon them
3. Father against son
4. A just leader (ruler)
5. A good person
6. A good child for his parents
7. A traveler
8. A fasting person until he breaks his fast
9. A Muslim to a Muslim in abstentia
10. A Muslim who does not for an immediate answer from Allah (swt) or something that may harm another.
11. A person who comes to Allah (swt) with repentance
12. A person who makes Du`aa' with the greatest Names of Allah (swt).

Anytime Allah (swt) accepts your Du`aa', you should be grateful to Him by saying:

الْحَمْدُ لِلّٰهِ الَّذِيْ بِنِعْمَتِهِ تَتِمُّ الصَّالِحَاتُ

Praise be to Allah (swt) for ending our activities with His Blessings.

We should call upon Allah (swt) with all His Beautiful Names so that He will bless us. Allah (swt) says in Surah Al-Israa' (Night Travel), the following:

قُلِ ادْعُوا اللَّهَ أَوِ ادْعُوا الرَّحْمَٰنَ أَيًّا مَّا تَدْعُوا فَلَهُ الْأَسْمَاءُ الْحُسْنَىٰ وَلَا تَجْهَرْ بِصَلَاتِكَ وَلَا تُخَافِتْ بِهَا وَابْتَغِ بَيْنَ ذَٰلِكَ سَبِيلًا ۝

Say: Call upon Allah, or call upon Al Rahman: By whatever Name you call upon Him, (it is well): For to Him belong the Most Beautiful Names. Neither speak your prayer aloud, nor speak it in a low tone, but seek a middle course between. (17:110)

If anyone has lost their job and is over loaded with debts or if some one is not able to find a job in order to pay their loans, then the best Du`aa' to say is the following Du`aa' of the Prophet:

١ – رَوَى الترمذي وحسّنه عن علي رضي الله عنه، أنَّ مكاتباً جَاءَهُ. فقال:
إنِّي عَجَزْتُ عَنْ كِتَابَتِي فَأَعِنِّي . فَقَالَ : أَلاَ أُعَلِّمُكَ كَلِمَاتٍ عَلَّمَنِيهِنَّ رسول
الله صلى الله عليه وسلم لَوْكَانَ عَلَيْكَ مِثْلُ جَبَلٍ صَبِر [١] دَيْناً إِلاَّ أَدَّاهُ اللهُ عَنْكَ، قُلْ:
« أَللَّهُمَّ اكْفِنِي بِحَلالِكَ عَنْ حَرَامِكَ ، وَأَغْنِنِي بِفَضْلِكَ عَمَّنْ سِوَاكَ » .

O Allah! Make the halal sufficient for me rather than haram; and make me wealthy from your favors rather than from anyone else. (Tirmizi)

III. Position, Time and Place

The Position, the time and places where the Du`aa' is most likely to be accepted by Allah (swt) are the following:

1. During Sujud (Prostration)

2. The night before Friday and all day Friday

3. Between the Iqamah and start of Salat

4. Between the two Khutbas of Friday Congregation

5. The time when a Muslim army meets a non-Muslim army

6. When the rain is coming down

7. At the time of Sahar or pre-dawn

8. Lailatul Qadr or the Night of Power

9. The Day of Arafa, the day before Eid-ul-Adha

10. During the month Ramadan

11. After each Salat

123

12. When Muslims are gathering for Congregation

13. Wherever there is a get together for Zikr or the Remembrance of Allah (swt)

14. After drinking water of Zamzam

15. When closing the eyes of the deceased

16. Du`aa' during the easy life and then during difficulty

It should be mentioned here that nothing could change the decision of Allah (swt) when accepting a Du`aa'. The power of the Du`aa' is so important that Muslims should benefit from it.

IV. Final Remarks

It is a good idea to reflect on this topic with the following Hadith Qudsi from our beloved Prophet Muhammad (pbuh) who reported it on behalf of Allah (swt):

٥ – وروى أبو يعلى عن أنس عن النبي صلى الله عليه وسلم فيما يرويه
عن ربه عز وجل ، قال : « أربع خصال : واحدة منهن لي ، وواحدة لك ،
وواحدة فيما بيني وبينك ، وواحدة فيما بيني وبين عبادي . فأما الذي لي
لا تشرك بي شيئاً ، وأما الذي لك ، فما عملت من خير جزيتك عليه ، وأما
الذي بيني وبينك ، فمنك الدعاء وعلي الإجابة . وأما الذي بيني وبين عبادي ،
فارض لهم ما ترضى لنفسك » .

There are four characteristics: one of which is for Me, one for you (people), one between Me and you, and one between you and My servants (people). The one for Me is that you don't associate anyone with Me; the one for you, is whatever you do good I will reward you for; the one between Me and you is that you make a Du`aa'

*and I am to answer it; and the one between you and My
servants is to be pleased for them similar to what you
want to be pleased for yourself. (Narrated by Anas)*

In order to benefit from what has been written about Du`aa',
let's try to improve our relationship with Allah (swt), and let's
keep in touch with Him for all days and all nights. We pray to
Allah (swt) to accept our Du`aa' Insha Allah. Ameen!

And Allah is the Best Sustenance

I. Introduction

Dear Muslims   **Assalamu `Alaikum**

Du`aa' is a supplication between us, the people, and Allah (swt), the Creator. Because we need Allah (swt), we should ask for His help, guidance, and forgiveness for our mistakes. Allah (swt) created everything in the Universe. He taught us what to do and how to do it. He also taught us how to communicate with Him. Further, He showed us how the Prophets and Messengers communicated with their Lord and how they used to supplicate.

In this chapter, I'd like to illustrate many of the supplications (Du`aa') that were made by our beloved Prophets. Sometimes, the Du`aa' is answered immediately by Allah (swt) and sometimes it may take time for its wisdom to be revealed.

II. Du`aa' of Prophet Zakaria

Prophet Zakaria and his wife did not have children. They were taking care of baby Mariam. They became old and Prophet Zakaria made a Du`aa' to Allah (swt).

Allah (swt) may chose to accept the Du`aa' momentarily or He may chose to delay the response. In this case, Allah (swt) accepted the Du`aa' of Prophet Zakariya immediately while he was still praying in the mosque. Allah (swt) gave him the glad tidings of an offspring by the name of Yahiya, who will one day be a Prophet. In Surah Al-Imran, the Qur'an states the following:

هُنَالِكَ دَعَا زَكَرِيَّا رَبَّهُ قَالَ رَبِّ هَبْ لِي مِن لَّدُنكَ ذُرِّيَّةً طَيِّبَةً إِنَّكَ سَمِيعُ الدُّعَاءِ ۝ فَنَادَتْهُ الْمَلَئِكَةُ وَهُوَ قَائِمٌ يُصَلِّي فِي الْمِحْرَابِ أَنَّ اللَّهَ يُبَشِّرُكَ بِيَحْيَى مُصَدِّقًا بِكَلِمَةٍ مِّنَ اللَّهِ وَسَيِّدًا وَحَصُورًا وَنَبِيًّا مِّنَ الصَّالِحِينَ ۝

126

There did Zakariya pray to his Lord, saying: "O my Lord! Grant unto me from You a progeny that is pure: for You hears prayer!" While he was standing in prayer in the chamber, the angels called unto him: "Allah does give you glad tidings of Yahya, confirming the truth of a Word from Allah, and (be Besides) noble, chaste And a Prophet- Of the (goodly) company of the righteous". (3:38-39)

III. Du`aa' of Prophet Ibrahim

While discussing the topic of Du`aa', we want to make sure that one doesn't expect every Du`aa' to be answered immediately in the same way and in the same method in which it was asked. Remember that Allah (swt) knows what is best for you and He knows when is the best time for you to have what you have asked for. Sometimes, the answer may come to you before you even open your mouth and other times it may be a delayed answer. We have to remember that the answer may even be delayed until after death. It is He alone, Allah (swt), who knows what is best for you and when and how to answer your Du`aa'.

Remember that Prophet Ibrahim asked Allah (swt) to grant him offspring from his son, Isma'il, who would call all the people to worship Allah (swt). Prophet Ibrahim made his famous Du`aa' after he brought his son Isma'il to Makkah from Palestine. In Surah Ibrahim (Ibrahim), Allah (swt) says the following about Prophet Ibrahim and his son Isma'il:

رَّبَّنَآ إِنِّى أَسْكَنتُ مِن ذُرِّيَّتِى بِوَادٍ غَيْرِ ذِى زَرْعٍ عِندَ بَيْتِكَ ٱلْمُحَرَّمِ رَبَّنَا لِيُقِيمُوا ٱلصَّلَوٰةَ فَٱجْعَلْ أَفْئِدَةً مِّنَ ٱلنَّاسِ

تَهْوِىٓ إِلَيْهِمْ وَٱرْزُقْهُم مِّنَ ٱلثَّمَرَٰتِ لَعَلَّهُمْ يَشْكُرُونَ ۝

رَبَّنَآ إِنَّكَ تَعْلَمُ مَا نُخْفِى وَمَا نُعْلِنُ وَمَا يَخْفَىٰ عَلَى ٱللَّهِ مِن شَىْءٍ

فِى ٱلْأَرْضِ وَلَا فِى ٱلسَّمَآءِ ۝ ٱلْحَمْدُ لِلَّهِ ٱلَّذِى وَهَبَ لِى

عَلَى ٱلْكِبَرِ إِسْمَٰعِيلَ وَإِسْحَٰقَ إِنَّ رَبِّى لَسَمِيعُ ٱلدُّعَآءِ ۝

رَبِّ ٱجْعَلْنِى مُقِيمَ ٱلصَّلَوٰةِ وَمِن ذُرِّيَّتِى رَبَّنَا وَتَقَبَّلْ

دُعَآءِ ۝

"O Our Lord! I have made some of my offspring to dwell in a valley without cultivation, by Your Sacred House; in order, O our Lord, that they may establish regular Prayer: so fill the hearts of some among men with love towards them, and feed them with fruits: so that they may give thanks. O our Lord! Truly You do know what we conceal and what we reveal: For nothing whatever is hidden from Allah, whether on earth or in heaven. Praise be to Allah. Who has granted unto me in old age Isma'il and Isaac: for truly My Lord is He, the Hearer of Prayer! O my Lord! Make me one who establishes regular Prayer, and also (raise such) among my offspring O our Lord! And You accept my prayer."
(14:37-40)

In Surah Al-Baqarah (The Cow), Allah (swt) makes reference to another Du`aa' of Prophet Ibrahim as follows:

رَبَّنَا وَٱبْعَثْ فِيهِمْ رَسُولًا ۝

مِّنْهُمْ يَتْلُواْ عَلَيْهِمْ ءَايَٰتِكَ وَيُعَلِّمُهُمُ ٱلْكِتَٰبَ وَٱلْحِكْمَةَ

وَيُزَكِّيهِمْ إِنَّكَ أَنتَ ٱلْعَزِيزُ ٱلْحَكِيمُ ۝

"Our Lord! Send amongst them A Messenger of their own, who shall rehearse Your Signs to them and instruct them in Scripture and Wisdom, and purify them: For You are the Exalted in Might, the Wise." *(2:129)*

Allah (swt) heard the Du`aa' of Prophet Ibrahim and He answered his Du`aa'; however, the answer did not manifest itself until 3,000 years later, after Prophet Ibrahim's death, when Prophet Muhammad (pbuh) was born into Makkah, the Arabian Peninsula. So you can see here that Allah (swt) answers the Du`aa' of his servants but He decides what, when and how to execute the His answer. Therefore, we are left to understand that it is our duty and our responsibility to call upon Allah (swt) but how He answers our Du`aa' is completely left up to Him to answer the way He wishes and at the time He finds suitable for us.

Allah is Beautiful, He Likes Beauty;
Prophet says the truth.

I. Introduction

Dear Muslims

Assalamu `Alaikum

At the onset of a community meeting or gathering, many times, mayors and/or city councilmen will invite religious leaders to give an invocation with a short prayer (supplication) so that God (Allah) will bless and guide them to work for the good and benefit of their communities. These religious leaders should be neutral in their approach. He/she should make supplication without using special words or statements from his religious denomination or even from his religion. The prayer should be a universal one, which is applicable and not offensive to any religion, and should not exceed 3 to 5 minutes.

When a Muslim is invited to give an invocation, he should be very careful and know what to say and how to say it. There is no need to mention the name Allah (swt), the name God is more universal. There is no need to refer to Islam, Muslims, Qur'an, Hadith and so on. It is enough that you are a Muslim Speaker and you have a Muslim name. They already know that you represent an Islamic Center. Enough is enough. The following are examples of 3 different varieties of invocations that may be given:

II. Speech (Invocation)

A. City of Diamond Bar

ISLAMIC EDUCATION CENTER
659 Brea Canyon Rd. Suite #2 , Walnut, CA 91789
Phone: (909) 594-1310   Fax: (909) 444-0832
e-mail: ahmadsakr@yahoo.com website:ahmadsakr.com

INVOCATION
City of Diamond Bar
Ahmad H. Sakr, Director

June 19, 2007

Your Honor: The Mayor of the City
Your Excellencies the Members of the City Council &
Their Staff Members
The Honorable members of the Sheriff & Fire Departments
The Respected Delegates and Representatives of the Community
Leaders

Ladies and Gentlemen:

We've gathered here today to pray for the guidance, success and happiness of our Leaders: O God, You are the Creator of the Universe, The Most Beneficent and Most Merciful, please grant guidance, success and happiness to our Mayor, to the Members of the City Council, to all of their staff members and to all of their advisors.

While we are gathered here in peace and harmony, we pray to God to protect us all from natural disasters. We pray for the sick, for the homeless and for the less fortunate. We pray for peace, justice and fairness for everybody in the world irrespective of color, nationality, gender or religion, whether we are Republicans or Democrats, after all we are American first, and we are one Nation under God with Liberty and Justice for all. After all, we are all the children of Adam and Eve. O God! You created all of us with love and Mercy. We should love each other, respect one another, and accept our diversity as a Bouquet of different flowers with good aroma. Please put in the hearts of everyone love and mercy so that we can live a better life.

Ladies and Gentlemen:

We pray to God to guide us to work together so that we will be able to protect our neighborhoods from gangs, drug dealers, taggers, shootings, killings, and drunk drivers. We pray to God to help us improve the environment in our schools, whereby the children and youth will respect the teachers, the administrators, the elders, their parents and the officials in charge. Students of today are the future leaders of America. Members of the Sheriff and Fire Departments are working very hard to protect us all, and to bring peace and happiness to our community. We are grateful to them and we pray for their safety and for their happiness.

Let us reflect on the name of our city "Diamond Bar". It is a beautiful name. It denotes diamonds in its purity. We, residents of Diamond Bar, should represent the purity of the name, its richness and its value. Each citizen is a valuable asset to the city, and every one should display richness in their character and behavior. So let's work together to keep Diamond Bar the purest and the richest city in America.

Last but not least, we pray to God to help us render our service to our leaders as volunteers so that they will be able to achieve their goals. God bless those who are here today. God bless **America**. God bless **The Whole World**. Amen!

B.   **City of La Mirada**

Muslim Community Services, Inc.
15077 Imperial Hwy, La Mirada, CA 90638

INVOCATION
City of La Mirada
By: Dr. Ahmad H. Sakr

October 23, 2007

Your Honor: The Mayor of the City
Your Excellencies the Members of the City Council &
Their Staff Members
The Honorable members of the Sheriff & Fire Departments, The respected Religious Leaders, The Respected Delegates and Representatives of the Community Leaders

Ladies and Gentlemen:

We came here today to pray for guidance, success and happiness for our Leaders: We wish to pray: O God, You are the Creator of the Universe, The Most Beneficent and Most Merciful, please grant guidance, success and happiness to our Mayor, to the Members of the City Council, to all their staff members, and to all their advisors. Moreover, we pray to God to protect us all from natural disasters. We pray for the sick, for the homeless and for the less fortunate. We pray for peace, justice and fairness for everybody in the world irrespective of color, nationality, gender or religion whether we are Republicans or Democrats, we are Americans first, and we are one Nation under God with Liberty and Justice for all. Further, we are all the children of Adam and Eve. We say: O God! You created all of us with Love and Mercy. Please put in everyone's hearts love, mercy, honor, dignity and respect, so that we can live a better life. We should love each other, respect one another, and accept our diversity as a Bouquet of

133

different flowers with good aroma. We pray for the members of the Sheriff and Fire Departments for their safety and happiness. They are working very hard to protect us all, and to bring peace and happiness to our community. We are grateful to them.

Ladies and Gentlemen:

As you all know, **Dr. Martin Luther King Jr.** had a Dream. We, as Americans, also have a Dream, a Hope, a Vision, and an Action that we'd like to see fulfilled. Therefore, we pray to God to inspire each and every one of us to go out and extend a helping hand to those who are less fortunate than we are. By doing so, God will give credit and blessings to those who sacrifice and deny themselves for the sake of those who are truly in need.

Mr. George Washington, the first President of the United States, said in his farewell speech in 1796 that we Americans should not entangle ourselves with foreign countries and foreign policies. America should take care of its local citizens. Charity starts at home first and foremost.

Let us also remember what **Mr. John F. Kennedy**, former US president said: "And so my fellow Americans, ask not what your country can do for you, ask what you can do for your country." Therefore we request God to inspire each one of us who are here, to offer their services Free to the Mayor and to the City Council members so as to improve our city. **God Bless you all, God Bless America, and God bless the whole World. Ameen!**

C.   City of Walnut

ISLAMIC EDUCATION CENTER
659 Brea Canyon Rd. Suite #2 , Walnut, CA 91789
Phone: (909) 594-1310   Fax: (909) 444-0832
e-mail: drahmadsakr@yahoo.com website:ahmadsakr.com

INVOCATION

City of Walnut
Ahmad H. Sakr, Director

June 25, 2008

Your Honor
Your Excellencies, the Members of the City Council, Mayor
Pro tem
The Respected Staff Members
The Honorable members of the Sheriff & Fire Departments
The Respected Delegates and Representatives of the Community
Leaders

Ladies and Gentlemen:

We've gathered here today to pray for the guidance, success and happiness of our Leaders: O God, You are the Creator of the Universe, The Most Beneficent and Most Merciful, please grant guidance, success and happiness to our Mayor, to the Members of the City Council, to all their staff members, to their advisors, and to all the ladies and gentlemen who are here today attending this session.

While we gather here in peace and harmony, we pray to God to protect us all from natural disasters. We pray for the sick, for the homeless and for the less fortunate. We pray for peace, justice and fairness for everybody in the world irrespective of color, nationality, gender, or religion, whether we are Republicans or Democrats, after all we are Americans first, and we are one Nation under God with Liberty and Justice for all. We are all the children of Adam and Eve. O God! You created all of us with love and Mercy. We should love each other, respect one another, and accept our diversity as a Bouquet of different flowers with good aroma. Please put in everyone's hearts love and mercy so that we can live a better life.

Ladies and Gentlemen:

We pray to God to guide us to work together so that we will be able to protect our neighborhoods from gangs, drug dealers, taggers, shootings, killings and drunk drivers. We pray to God to help us improve the environment in our schools, whereby the children and youth will respect the teachers, the administrators, the elders, their parents and the officials in charge. Students of today will be the future leaders of America tomorrow. Members of the Sheriff and Fire Departments are working very hard to protect us all, and to bring peace and happiness to our community. We are grateful to them and we pray for their safety and happiness.

Ladies and Gentlemen:

Let us remember the words of Mr. John F. Kennedy, former president of the United States of America. He said, "And so my fellow Americans, ask not what your country can do you for; ask what you can do for your country." We request God to inspire each and every one of us here today to offer their services Free to the Mayor and the City Council members so as to improve our city and our quality of life. **God Bless you all, God Bless America and God bless the whole World. Ameen!**

I. Introduction

When the community wants to build a Masjid, a school or any other facility, they'll start off by inviting friends and some city officials for a Ground Breaking event. This program will mark the start of the building of the facility after being granted the Zoning Permits from the City Hall. A few individuals will be invited to say few words and then they'll ask the guests to go out and start digging in to the soil, as if they're going to build the structure at that moment.   The wisdom behind asking the guests to start digging is that they want each person to get credit with Allah (swt) for assuming a part in helping in the construction to build this facility that will benefit the community.   In the process, each person will praise the name of Allah (swt) and ask Him to bless the Institute and those who are in charge of running it.

II. Speech

Dear Brothers and Sisters
Assalamu `Alaikum

Let me greet you by saying Assalamu `Alaikum. We are thankful first and foremost to Allah (swt) Who created us with love and mercy and bestowed upon us knowledge and wisdom. He taught us what to say and what not to say.

We are grateful to those who have invited us to partake in this noble occasion, which will commence the building of the House of Allah (swt), the Masjid. Allah (swt) has encouraged Muslims to build Masajid and to take care of them. In Surah Al-Tawbah (Repentance), Allah (swt) says the following:

إِنَّمَا يَعْمُرُ مَسَٰجِدَ ٱللَّهِ مَنْ ءَامَنَ بِٱللَّهِ وَٱلْيَوْمِ ٱلْءَاخِرِ وَأَقَامَ ٱلصَّلَوٰةَ وَءَاتَى ٱلزَّكَوٰةَ وَلَمْ يَخْشَ إِلَّا ٱللَّهَ فَعَسَىٰ أُوْلَٰٓئِكَ أَن يَكُونُوا۟ مِنَ ٱلْمُهْتَدِينَ ۝

The mosques of Allah shall be visited and maintained by such as believe in Allah and the Last Day, establish regular prayers, and practice regular charity, and fear none (at all) except Allah. It is they who are expected to be on true guidance. (9:18)

Dear Brothers and Sisters

Whoever builds a House of Worship (Masjid) on this planet, Allah (swt) will build for him a House in Paradise.

The Prophet (pbuh) said the following about mosques:

Narrated by Uthman Ibn Affan (May Allah be pleased with him), that the Prophet (pbuh) said:

عَنْ عُثْمَانَ رَضِيَ اللهُ عَنْهُ، أنَّ النَّبِيَّ صَلَّى اللهُ عَلَيْهِ وَسَلَّمَ قال:
«مَنْ بَنَى لِلّٰهِ مَسْجِداً يَبْتَغِي بِهِ وَجْهَ اللّٰهِ، بَنَى اللّٰهُ لَهُ بَيْتاً فِي الْجَنَّةِ.»

— متفق عليه —

Whoever builds a mosque for Allah (swt) with the intention to please Him, Allah (swt) will build him a house in paradise. Agreed

III. Final Remarks

Since we were chosen by Allah (swt) to be the witnesses for this Ground Breaking event for the Masjid, then we should do whatever we can, either in the form of money, time or services, to help this local community get this House of Allah (swt) built as soon as possible.

Dear Friends

Your credits are with Allah (swt). For every dollar you spend on this project, you will get 700% compounded capital return on a daily basis. This means that the one dollar you spend now is equal to $700 today. Tomorrow will be $1400; the day after $2,800; and the day after is $5,600; and it goes on and on and on.

Dear Brothers and Sisters

A Ground Breaking is the first step in getting the community involved and committed. Let us pray to Allah (swt) that such a project will be materialized soon with the help and support of all of us. Ameen! Thank you all.

There is no deity except Allah
Muhammad is the Messenger of Allah

Chapter (39)	Fund Raising

I. General

Muslims everywhere in the world will gather to try to raise funds to build institutions, such as Masajid, schools, clinics, hospitals, orphanages, and so on. Most often, the organizers will try to raise money within their own local communities and other times the leaders may have to travel from country to country or from city to city. In order a fundraising function to be successful, the community organizers should organize themselves ahead of time before the function takes place. They should invite all the members of the community as well as their Muslim neighbors of other Islamic community centers.

The program should be well organized and should be short and to the point. In order to have a good turnout, you should invite a speaker that is well known as a scholar and who has experience with Fund Raising events. The speaker should be well informed about the local community and the project for which he will be fund raising for. He should know how to begin and how to end the function.

II. Speech

Dear Brothers and Sisters

Assalamu `Alaikum

- Please say Takbeer: Allahu Akbar
- We are thankful to Allah (swt) to be invited to this function. We are thankful to all of you for participating in this noble and sacred cause. We are also thankful to those friends who have organized this program and invited all of us here today.

Dear Brothers and Sisters

We did not gather here today for the purpose of eating together. The food is available and Insha Allah we will all have our meal later. We also did not come here to watch like bystanders but rather we are here to take action. We did not come here today to socialize although we have been socializing. We came here today for the sole purpose of raising enough money to build this House of Worship, the Masjid. It is the House of Allah (swt), a.k.a. Bait of Allah. As you know, Allah loves you and He inspired you to leave your houses and your businesses today to come here. You came here because Allah (swt) is the One Who invited you to come here. So be grateful and thankful to Allah (swt) that He invited you here so that you may invest with Him, in the Bank of Allah (swt). Allah (swt) wants you to invest now, not tomorrow. We do not know whether we'll be alive tomorrow or not. Therefore, each one of us needs to invest as much as they can now before it's too late. If you invest now you will be the winner in this world and the hereafter. You need to build this House of Allah (swt) so that Allah (swt) will build you a House in Paradise.

Dear Friends

Your donation counts as a Sadaqa (charity). This Sadaqa will protect you from (70) different crisis's from happening to you. So protect yourself from calamities by giving Sadaqa in the way of Allah (swt). Moreover, if you are sick, give Sadaqa before going to the doctor. Then Allah (swt) will give you a speedy recovery and good health. Remember brothers and sisters, the more you invest with Allah (swt) today, the sooner you will get a return on your money from some unknown and unexpected source. Allah (swt) will replace your donation with more and more in this life and even more in the hereafter. Now it is up to you to do what you want. Keep in mind that your donations are tax deductible with IRS because this masjid is registered as a non-profit organization.

III. Final Remarks

Dear Friends

Your donation could be any of the following:

1. Cash
2. Checks
3. Pledges
4. Credit cards
5. Zakat
6. Sadaqa
7. Loan
8. Bank to Bank wire or transfer
9. On behalf of your parents
10. Matching dollar for dollar
11. Living Trust
12. Other and other

Therefore, let us start collecting the funds that are needed for this very important cause. And further, I ask Allah (swt) to bless you and reward you two fold for your generous contributions. Ameen!

Allah Al-Mu'min, Al-Muhaymin, Al-'Aziz,
Al-Jabbar, Al-Mutakabbir

I. Introduction

Assalamu 'Alaikum

It is very exciting to be invited to speak to a group of non-Muslims and to be able to share our faith with them. Muslim speakers need to be careful of what to say, how to say it, and for how long to speak. It's possible that you may be invited to speak to non-Muslim students at a college or university; or to adults in an interfaith session at a church or synagogue; more so, it could be at the city hall in front of the Mayor and/or city councilmen. Some non-Muslims may wish to visit you and the Muslim community at the mosque during the Friday Khutbah and Salat, or at any other time during the week.

Regardless of the occasion, the speaker must know what is and what is not appropriate to say. He should also be sensitive to the way he says things and for how long he speaks. It could be that more than one person wishes to speak, or to ask questions. You must be accommodating. This is a golden opportunity for a Muslim Da'iyah to deliver the Message of Allah (swt) to large numbers of people. First, we should welcome the guests and thank them all for coming in addition to thanking the coordinator of the group. We should then offer them refreshments, snacks and/or lunch or dinner. We should distribute literature and books to them about Islam free of charge. And last, we should make sure that some our Muslim friends are also attending the function for support. The supporters should be sensitive to the feelings of their guests of other faiths.

II. General Speech

One idea for a general introduction would be to say, "We are here today Not to Convert... Proselytize... Baptize ...Teach... Debate or convince anyone. We are here to share our common values and common beliefs. We have more things in common than we may be aware of and I would like to spend our time sharing such things. I do not want to talk now about theology, but rather about Family Values and those who are Homeless, Refugees, Sick, Out-of-job, and many more. I am sure God will be pleased with us if we join together with solidarity and try to resolve the problems and help those who are less fortunate.

Ladies and Gentlemen

Welcome! We welcome each and every one of you by saying Assalamu `Alaikum, which means Peace Be Upon you. Muslims greet each other everyday with this greeting of Peace so that we may live peacefully with each other. However, the Source of Peace comes from God (Allah). One of the Most Beautiful Names of Allah (swt) is that He is the Peace; Assalaam.

Further, when we address each other, either personally or in a group, we say and refer to one another as Brothers and Sisters. This means that we respect and honor each other as if we were biological brothers and sisters.

Therefore, my dear Brothers/Sisters, we aim to Dialogue with one another and not Debate. We try to learn from each other and learn about the diverse backgrounds of each other. We are taught to seek knowledge and wisdom throughout our lives from the cradle to the grave. It is not enough to just seek knowledge because without the application of wisdom, our knowledge would end up in a horrible catastrophe.

Ladies and Gentlemen... Brothers and Sisters

Islam is the religion of Peace. Muslims believe in the Oneness of God, whose name is Allah; The One and Only God. They believe in all the previous prophets and messengers of Allah (swt) that were sent to all the people of the world until the Day of Judgment.

The basic pillars of Islam are five as follows:

(1) Declaration of Faith
(2) Praying five times a day
(3) Fasting the month of Ramadan (9th lunar calendar month)
(4) Paying Zakat 2.5% after expenses
(5) Performing pilgrimage to Makkah once in their lifetime if they can afford it.

The pillars of Faith are six as follows:

(1) Belief in the Oneness of God
(2) Belief in the Angels
(3) Belief in the Books revealed by God
(4) Belief in the Prophets and Messengers
(5) Belief in The Day of Judgment, and
(6) Belief in our Destiny

III. Final Remarks

Ladies and Gentlemen... Brothers and Sisters

We want to thank you for visiting with us. We hope we will have more occasions to visit with each other and to get to know one another in the near future. By doing so, we will be able to work together as pioneers to improve our society. And most importantly, Allah (swt) will be most pleased with us. May Allah (swt) bless you and May Allah bless the whole world. Ameen!

If there is anything we can do to be of assistance, please don't hesitate to ask. We will be available after the session for anyone who may have some questions. Again, thanks for coming.

Chapter (41)   Marriage Officiations

I. General

Assalamu `Alaikum

We are thankful first and foremost to Allah (swt). Second, we are thankful to the two families who invited us to officiate the marriage of their son and daughter. I am sure the young couple is happy to get married today, however; in Islam, marriage is not only between the young couple, but between the two families who have joined together to establish a single family (`Aa-ilah). The bride has to have a Wakeel (Guardian) who represents her interest. There should also be two witnesses present, one from each side of the family. The groom should offer a Mahr (Dowry) to the bride, one in advance, prior to the wedding, and another to be given at a later date during their lifetime. It is recommended that the groom give a wedding ring to the bride as a sign of responsibility.

Ladies and Gentlemen: As far as the registration of the marriage is concerned, the young couples need to go to the Family Department of the Court House and request them to officiate their marriage.   However, they should tell them that our Religious Leader is going to officiate our marriage. They'll need to fill half of the certificate and we will fill the other half. Also, we will fill the Islamic papers according to Islamic Shari'ah (Jurisprudence). We'll make four copies of the marriage document; one for the bride, one for the groom, and the third will be sent back to the State to register the marriage of the couple. The last copy of the document will be on file with the Masjid.

II. Khitbatul Nikah

Dear Friends:

Before officiating the marriage of the young couple, I would like to offer Khitbah Nikah. Bismillah... Walhamdu Lillah...

Walaa Ilaaha Illa-Allah. Allah (swt) revealed a Surah in the Qur'an titled An-Nisaa' (The Women). Allah (swt) says the following:

بِسۡمِ اللهِ الرَّحۡمٰنِ الرَّحِيۡمِ

يَـٰٓأَيُّهَا ٱلنَّاسُ ٱتَّقُوا۟ رَبَّكُمُ ٱلَّذِى خَلَقَكُم مِّن نَّفۡسٍ وَٰحِدَةٍ وَخَلَقَ مِنۡهَا زَوۡجَهَا وَبَثَّ مِنۡهُمَا رِجَالًا كَثِيرًا وَنِسَآءً وَٱتَّقُوا۟ ٱللَّهَ ٱلَّذِى تَسَآءَلُونَ بِهِۦ وَٱلۡأَرۡحَامَ إِنَّ ٱللَّهَ كَانَ عَلَيۡكُمۡ رَقِيبًا ١

O mankind! Fear your guardian Lord Who created you from a single person, created out of it his mate and from them twain scattered like seeds countless men and women. Fear Allah, through Whom you demand your mutual rights, and be heedful of the wombs that bore you: for Allah ever watches over you. (4:1)

Also, Allah (swt) says in Surah Al-Room the following:

وَمِنۡ ءَايَـٰتِهِۦٓ أَنۡ خَلَقَ لَكُم مِّنۡ أَنفُسِكُمۡ أَزۡوَٰجًا لِّتَسۡكُنُوٓا۟ إِلَيۡهَا وَجَعَلَ بَيۡنَكُم مَّوَدَّةً وَرَحۡمَةً إِنَّ فِى ذَٰلِكَ لَءَايَـٰتٍ لِّقَوۡمٍ يَتَفَكَّرُونَ ٢١

And among His Signs is this, that He created for your mates from among yourselves, that you may dwell in tranquility with them, and He has put love and mercy between your (hearts): Verily in that are Signs for those who reflect. (30:21)

Dear Brothers and Sisters: Our prophet (pbuh) said:

Our Prophet (pbuh) said:

O young men! Whoever can assume the responsibility should get married as soon as possible. It will help him to cast down his eyes, and protect his private organ; otherwise, he should fast so as to control his sex appetite.

A woman may be married for one of four reasons; for her beauty, for her position, for her wealth, or for her piety. Get married to the Pious one, you will be blessed.

May Allah (swt) bless you both. May Allah (swt) help you live together with happiness. May Allah (swt) grant you good and righteous offspring. Ameen!

Let us read Al-Fatiha (The Opening);

In the name of Allah, Most Gracious, Most Merciful

Praise be to Allah The cherisher and sustainer of the worlds; Most Gracious; Most Merciful; Master of the Day of Judgment; You do we worship; And Your aid we seek. Show us the straight way; The way of those on whom You have bestowed Your Grace Those whose (portion) is not wrath And who go not astray. (1:1-7)

Chapter (42)	Mother's Day

I. Introduction

Dear Muslims

Assalamu `Alaikum

Many people in different parts of the world celebrate Mother's Day. It only comes around once every year. In USA, Mother's Day is celebrated each year on the second Sunday in the month of May. On this day, usually people are concerned with trying to please their own mothers and the mother's within their own family. Sometimes, children, relatives, and friends may greet the mother's of strangers. What we should know is that Allah (swt) has blessed mothers all over the world and throughout history. In Surah Al-Ahqaaf (Winding Sand-tracts), Allah (swt) says the following:

وَوَصَّيْنَا ٱلْإِنسَٰنَ بِوَٰلِدَيْهِ إِحْسَٰنًا حَمَلَتْهُ أُمُّهُ كُرْهًا وَوَضَعَتْهُ كُرْهًا وَحَمْلُهُ وَفِصَٰلُهُ ثَلَٰثُونَ شَهْرًا حَتَّىٰٓ إِذَا بَلَغَ أَشُدَّهُ وَبَلَغَ أَرْبَعِينَ سَنَةً قَالَ رَبِّ أَوْزِعْنِىٓ أَنْ أَشْكُرَ نِعْمَتَكَ ٱلَّتِىٓ أَنْعَمْتَ عَلَىَّ وَعَلَىٰ وَٰلِدَىَّ وَأَنْ أَعْمَلَ صَٰلِحًا تَرْضَىٰهُ وَأَصْلِحْ لِى فِى ذُرِّيَّتِىٓ إِنِّى تُبْتُ إِلَيْكَ وَإِنِّى مِنَ ٱلْمُسْلِمِينَ ۝ أُو۟لَٰٓئِكَ ٱلَّذِينَ نَتَقَبَّلُ عَنْهُمْ أَحْسَنَ مَا عَمِلُوا۟ وَنَتَجَاوَزُ عَن سَيِّـَٔاتِهِمْ فِىٓ أَصْحَٰبِ ٱلْجَنَّةِ وَعْدَ ٱلصِّدْقِ ٱلَّذِى كَانُوا۟ يُوعَدُونَ ۝

We have enjoined on man kindness to his parents: In pain did his mother bear him, and in pain did she give him birth. The carrying of the (child) to his weaning is (a period of) thirty months. At length, when he reaches the age of full strength and attains forty years, He says, "O my Lord! Grant me that I may be grateful for Your favors which You have bestowed upon me, and upon both my parents, and that I may work righteous good deeds, such as please You; And make my offspring good. Truly have I turned to You and truly do I submit (To You) in Islam. Such are they from whom We shall accept the best of their deeds and pass by their ill deeds: (they shall Be) among the Companions of the Garden: a promise of truth, which was made to them (in this life). (46: 15-16)

II. Paradise at the Feet of the Mothers

Once it was said: "Mother is an institution by herself and she is a leader-maker." She knows how to mold and train her own children in the best way. She does this better than fathers and better than any baby-sitter.

While we celebrate Mother's Day, we should recognize that the mother is the backbone of a stable family and a good society. Mothers, in the home, keep the family together. With their love, affection, sympathy, mercy, trust, patience, and sacrifice they deserve to be honored and respected by all of us.

We salute all the mothers who have taken care of their children, have raised them with honor and dignity, and have trained them to be good leaders in America or any other part of the world. We need more mothers in our societies to dedicate their lives to taking care of their own children. No one should leave this noble responsibility for another person to do.

No other part of the society can do what a mother can do for her own children. No school, law enforcement, court decision, rehabilitation center or any other organization can replace or even be compared to the institute of a Mother. It is the mother who conceived and accepted the challenge of pregnancy for nine months. She suffered through the difficulties of morning sickness, labor pains, and childbirth. She nurtured her child with tenderness and care until the child grew up and became a grown person.

Mothers deserve to be honored and respected not only once a year, on Mother's Day, but every moment of her existence. Every child, young or old, male or female, should salute his/her mother daily for the sacrifices that she undertakes during the course of her child's life. For these reasons and many more, mothers deserve to be in Paradise; and Paradise is humble enough to make itself under the feet of your mother. It is said that, **"Paradise is at the Feet of Mothers."**

III. Final Remarks

Ladies and Gentlemen/ Brothers and Sisters

The topic of Mother's Day really brings us a golden opportunity to discuss the importance of our mothers in Islam and to be able to share it with other people from different societies. We pray to Allah (swt) to improve the society that we live in and to increase and share our happiness with one another. We thank you all and God bless you all. Ameen!

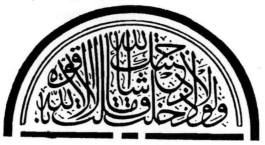

When you went to your garden, you should have said: There is no power but with Allah... Qur'an (18:39)

151

I.   Introduction

Dear Muslims

Assalamu `Alaikum

In order to get married, one must go through the process of Nikah (officiating legal marriage). The two families give their consent to their children; for the son of one family to marry the daughter of the other family so that they may establish a new family. The rules and regulations should be followed and executed accordingly. The daughter should heed the advice of her mother and learn how to live in peace and harmony with the groom after they are married.

In Islam, a society will not have a solid foundation unless it is built with good families that know how to give and take and know how to show mutual love, mercy, consultation, kindness, honor, respect, dignity and humbleness. It is a two way street.

II. A Mother's Advice to her daughter at Marriage

When `Amr son of Hujr, the king of Kinda, proposed to Om Iyas, daughter of 'Awaf, son of Mahallem Al Shibani, her mother Imamah, daughter of Harith, advised her daughter privately on what she should do to promote a happy marriage life and what she should do for her husband. She told her the following:

Oh daughter, if advice was better than politeness, I would have left it to you. But, it is the reminder to those who forget and a help to the wise ones.

If a woman does not need the financial support of a husband because her parents are rich or they are in need of her help, then this is OK. However, know that Allah (swt) has created women for men as He has created men for women.

Oh daughter, you will soon separate from this environment from which you grew up to go to a home that you are unfamiliar with and to join a mate that you are not used to. So, with his rights on you, he will be a watchful and earner of your rights. Be a woman to him and he will definitely become a slave to you.

Save for him ten characters and those characters will become your treasures:

As for the first and second, become respectful to him with conviction and listen and obey him in kindness.

As for the third and fourth, watch his eyes and nose, so he will not see any ugliness in you and will not smell but the best from you.

As for the fifth and sixth, watch for his times of sleep and of eat. The stress of hunger causes sizzling and the loss of sleepiness causes anger.

As for the seventh and eight, protect his wealth and his servings and his children. Good handling of his wealth is good appreciation and in his children good administration.

As for the ninth and ten, do not disobey him and reveal his secrets. If you disobey him, you would have hurt his heart and if you reveal his secrets you will not be safe from his bad reactions.

Then beware, never be in happiness before him when he is in sadness and never be in sadness in front of him when he is in happiness.

III. Final Remarks

Dear Muslims

It is widely recognized that Mothers are the best advisors to their children, especially to their daughters. A mother's advice to her children, sons and daughters alike, is just as important before they get married as it is after they get married. Therefore, we encourage all the daughters whose mothers are still alive to go and seek their advice. We pray to Allah (swt) to bless and reward all mothers and give them credit for their service in the hereafter. Ameen!

There is No Deity except Allah,
And Muhammad is the
Messenger Of Allah.

Chapter (44)	Waleemah

I. Introduction

Waleemah is a reception for the young couple after officiating their marriage. Some families will delay the Waleemah until the marriage has been consummated, i.e. the young couple has lived together and had marital relations. Other families may have two receptions; one at the time of marriage officiation and the other after the young couple join together. Some other families may have two different Waleemahs; one is done by the Groom's family and a few days later another Waleemah is done by the Bride's family. Muslim families may have different customs and traditions with respect to the Waleemah, however, nobody should criticize any family for doing it the wrong way.

The speaker should exercise wisdom on what to say on this occasion. He has to praise Allah (swt) first and then thank the families who organized the Waleemah. Finally, he should thank all those who attended the reception. The speaker needs to advise the young couple on how to live together and stay happy for the rest of their marriage life. The following is an example of a speech that could be delivered by the speaker to the people who are attending the Waleemah (reception):

II.   Waleemah Speech

Ladies and gentlemen / Brothers and Sisters

Assalamu `Alaikum.

We are very thankful to Allah (swt) that He has brought us together to share in the happiness of the young couple who got married today. The Waleemah reception is offered as a gesture of thanks and appreciation not only to the young couple but also to their families, relatives and all the friends that are attending the reception. The young couple should be thankful to Allah (swt) that they have living families, relatives and friends in this country. We make special Du`aa' for you Insha Allah.

Ladies and Gentlemen / Brothers and Sisters

Islam encourages everyone to get married as soon as they can. The young couple will receive many blessings from Allah (swt) by marrying young. Having marital relations between husband and wife is considered a form of worship and Ibadah to Allah (swt). It is a blessing if your parents are still alive. The beauty of the life cycle is a person is born, then they grow up, then they get married, then they have children, then the children grow up and have their own children. At this point, the child has grown up to be a grandfather or grandmother. The life cycle is now complete.

My message to the young couple is the following:

Try to stay together...Love each other...Respect each other. Consult each other before doing anything. Try to have good relations with both of your families, and relatives. Try to pray salat together ... Read Qur'an together and listen to Qur'anic recitation together... Try to save money and plan to perform Hajj together while you are young. Don't wait till you become a senior citizen. Visit many different Mosques and pray in them. Make sure that you attend Friday prayer at any mosque.

III.   Final Remarks

Ladies and Gentlemen / Brothers and Sisters

The Waleemah is a blessing from Allah (swt) for all of you who are here. Right now, the angels are taking pictures of everyone as witnesses and you are to be rewarded by Allah (swt). You came here to offer moral support to the families of the young couple, as well as to the young couple. May Allah (swt) bless you and reward you. The credits and blessings that you are getting are beyond imagination and beyond calculation.

Dear Friends

Our Du`aa' to the couple is the following:

May Allah (swt) bless the young couple; May Allah (swt) keep you together, and May Allah (swt) bless you with good children.

Ameen... Ameen... Ameen!

Let us read Surah Al-Fatiha (The Opening) together, the first chapter in the Qur'an. Thanks!

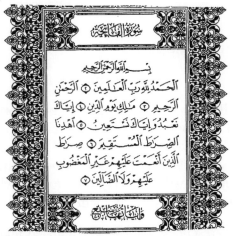

In the name of Allah, Most Gracious, Most Merciful

Praise be to Allah The cherisher and sustainer of the worlds; Most Gracious; Most Merciful; Master of the Day of Judgment; You do we worship; And Your aid we seek. Show us the straight way; The way of those on whom You have bestowed Your Grace Those whose (portion) is not wrath And who go not astray.   (1:1-7)

I. Introduction

The word `Aqeeqah in Arabic means a reception or celebration which is offered by the family after Allah (swt) has blessed them with the birth of a brand new baby. If the baby is born a girl, the family should sacrifice a lamb and invite their friends and relatives over for dinner. However, if the baby is born a boy, then the family should sacrifice two lambs and invite their friends and relatives over for dinner.

It is possible that the family may decide to invite a speaker or an Imam to the `Aqeeqah to say few words. The following is an example of a small speech that may be used for such an occasion:

II. Speech

Dear Brothers and Sisters

Assalamu `Alaikum

On behalf of the family and their new born, I would like to thank you all for coming to share in their happiness. Allah (swt) has blessed them with a new baby and this indeed is a blessing from Allah (swt). It is Allah (swt) who decides, in His infinite wisdom, whom He will grant children to and whom He will deny children to and whether to deny them temporarily or permanently.

Muslims are encouraged to get married and have children as soon as they possibly can. Having children and raising them as pious Muslims with the highest honor and dignity is the best investment one can make in life with Allah (swt). In doing so, our children will make Du`aa' for us and pay Sadaqa (charity) on our behalves after we die. These good deeds of our children will follow us parents to our graves. Indeed, this would be the best gift to us from Allah (swt).

Dear Friends

Immediately after birth, the parent should make the Azan in the baby's right ear and then make the Iqamah in the left ear. If the baby is a boy, then you should instruct the doctor to perform the circumcision as soon as possible. If it is a girl, circumcision is not required. Irrespective of the baby's gender, it is recommended to cut the baby's hair and give Sadaqah on behalf of the baby at the time of `Aqeeqah.

III. Final Remarks

Dear Brothers and Sisters

We, the parents, should raise our children to be pious Muslims with the highest honor and dignity. We should teach them how to behave with good manners and respect others. We should teach them how to make Salat, how to fast, how to read Qur'an, and how to listen to and memorize the Qur'an. We should teach them how to make Du`aa' so that they'll make du`aa' for us after our death; Ins-sha Allah. The best inheritance a parent can leave behind is a righteous child that makes du`aa' for them after their death. May Allah (swt) bless you all and may Allah (swt) bless the family that invited us to this `Aqeeqah. Allahumma Ameen!

I.　Introduction

Dear Muslims

Assalamu `Alaikum

Muslims are ordained by the Creator, Allah (swt), to seek knowledge from the cradle until the time of death. In Islam, a great emphasis is placed on seeking knowledge so as to avoid being ignorant. Ignorance is the source of a lot of trouble in the world. Those who are ignorant cannot and will not appreciate what Allah (swt) has created for them in the whole universe. Those who wish to remain ignorant are decreasing their status as a human being down to the level of animals. This means that they are abusing their intellectual power and destroying their thinking capacity.

In order to get rid of ignorance, one must seek knowledge. Knowledge can be sought from any place in the world and from any person in the world. However, knowledge in the absence of wisdom and humility may lead a person to catastrophe.

II.　Seeking Knowledge

Dear Muslims

True knowledge cannot be sought only by reading because without guidance, a person can very easily be misled with his own personal interpretations and his own understandings. One has to read and seek guidance and instruction from the knowledgeable scholars, teachers, and Imams. In the Qur'an, Allah (swt) instructed the faithful believers to seek knowledge from those who are knowledgeable. Allah (swt) says in Surah Al-Nahl (The Bees) the following:

وَمَا أَرْسَلْنَا مِنْ قَبْلِكَ إِلا رِجَالا نُوحِي إِلَيْهِمْ فَاسْأَلُوا أَهْلَ
الذِّكْرِ إِنْ كُنْتُمْ لا تَعْلَمُونَ

And before you We sent none but men to whom We granted inspiration. If you realize this not, ask of those who possess the Message. (16:43).

Dear Muslims

Having knowledge of the unseen world is more important than what we see in this world around us. People should do research and use advanced technology in order to be able to find out and see what is going on inside the living and the non-living beings. For those who try to seek knowledge with honesty and sincerity, they will be blessed by Allah (swt).

III.   Sources of Knowledge

The word knowledge ('ILM) is mentioned in the Qur'an more than 700 times in 87 different forms. In Surah Al-`Alaq (The Clot), it states the very first Ayat that were ever revealed to Prophet Muhammad (pbuh) when he was in Cave Hiraa'. Those Ayat refer to Allah's (swt) command to read by the One who created every person from sperm and ova to form the zygote. These Ayat are as follows:

اقْرَأْ بِاسْمِ رَبِّكَ الَّذِي خَلَقَ ـ خَلَقَ الإِنْسَانَ مِنْ عَلَقٍ ـ اقْرَأْ
وَرَبُّكَ الأَكْرَمُ ـ الَّذِي عَلَّمَ بِالْقَلَمِ ـ عَلَّمَ الإِنْسَانَ مَا لَمْ يَعْلَمْ

Read in the name of your Lord Who created- Created man, out of A (mere) clot Of congealed blood.

161

Read and your Lord is the Most Bounteous, Who taught by the pen, taught man that which he knew not. (96:1-5)

Prophet Muhammad (pbuh) emphasized 'ILM tremendously and encouraged Muslims to seek knowledge in any part of the world. The following hadith is narrated by Abu Hurairah ® that the Prophet (pbuh) said:

١٣٨٩ ـ وعن أبي هريرة رضي اللهُ عنه ، أن رسول الله ﷺ ، قال : « وَمَنْ سَلَكَ طَرِيقاً يَلْتَمِسُ فِيهِ عِلْماً ، سَهَّلَ اللهُ لَهُ طَرِيقاً إِلَى الْجَنَّةِ » رواه مسلم .

Any person, who follows the route for knowledge, Allah (swt) will make an easy way for him/her to paradise. [Reported by Muslim]

IV.   Final Remarks

It should be stated here that seeking knowledge through reading alone without receiving guidance from a teacher, an Imam, or a scholar could lead a person to erroneous interpretations and misunderstandings.   This is the very reason why we have Professor's, schools, colleges and universities. If we did not need instruction, then we wouldn't need to have professors at all! We could then just all sit at home and read books by ourselves only. Then we will be able to earn our own degrees in the areas of medical doctor, engineer, orator, artist, computer scientist, lawyer, judge, political scientist, pilot or any other profession.

It is important to note here that not every scholar has full knowledge of every field or even have all the details in his own field. It is possible that a scholar may be asked a question and he may not know the answer. In this case, he is required to seek the correct answer from other scholars as well as from outside reading.

I.   Introduction

Dear Muslims

Assalamu `Alaikum

Knowledge is just that, knowledge! Acquiring knowledge is good; however, the application of knowledge could either be good or bad. The application of knowledge in the absence of wisdom can lead a person to catastrophic circumstances, which will also have an affect on his fellowmen as well as on the society at large. It is possible that leaders may use and abuse their knowledge and destroy human beings just as the US did when they dropped an Atomic Bomb on Hiroshima and Nagasaki, Japan during the Second World War. Another example is some scientists, who have thought of themselves to be knowledgeable, will brag about themselves with arrogance, and try to destroy other honest scientists. They try to control others with hate and subjugation in order for them not to feel inferior. The story of Qaroon is a good example of a knowledgeable scientist who brags about himself and his background. You may read about Qaroon's story in the Qur'an, Surah Al-Qasas (The Narrations), chapter 28:76-83.

II. Wisdom From Allah

Dear Muslims

As is knowledge, one must realize that wisdom (Hikmah) is a gift from Allah (swt). It is Allah (swt) who gives wisdom to whomever He wishes. Anyone who has been granted wisdom should be grateful to Allah (swt) and should not brag about it. That person should pray daily and request from Allah (swt) to improve his wisdom, his knowledge, and his faith. Wise people know that they are not prophets and that they do not receive Revelation from Allah (swt). Therefore, they should be humble when acquiring knowledge and be willing to learn from the experiences of others. Further, speakers should understand how to apply the knowledge by knowing when, why, how, where and for how long to speak.

Dear Muslims

Allah (swt) has blessed us with two ears, two eyes and one mouth. Therefore, people should listen, look and think before they speak or say something that might be hurtful to others. Know that all of your speech is recorded by the two angels that sit on your shoulders. Even our intentions are being recorded. Accordingly one should be scared to utter a word just for the sake of talking unless you are saying something that is good. Allah (swt) informs us in the Qur'an in Surah An-Nisaa' (The Women) the following:

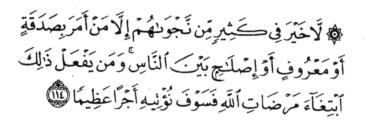

There is no good in most of their secret talks save (in) him who orders Sadaqah (charity in Allah's cause), or Ma'roof (Islamic Monotheism and all the good and righteous deeds which Allah has ordained), or conciliation between mankind; and he who does this, seeking the good Pleasure of Allah, We shall give him a great reward. (4:114)

III. Final Remarks

It is important to state that the Da'iyah must exercise wisdom when disseminating knowledge to others. He should know when, where, what, how, why and to whom he is talking and advising.

164

Therefore, in order to acquire wisdom, one must go back to Qur'an, Hadith, Sunnah, and the Sirah of the Prophet (pbuh) and his companions. One should attach themselves to a series of Muslims scholars and learn from their wisdom of knowledge. One should also learn how to practice what they have learned before preaching or delivering the wisdom. One has to recognize that seeking knowledge cannot only be done by reading alone. Even reading the wise words of others is not enough. One has to associate himself with those scholars who are wise, honest, sincere, and have demonstrated all these qualities in action without bragging about it. The older generations have already passed on their knowledge and wisdom to the next generation. Now it is up to the younger generation to benefit from the knowledge and wisdom of the elder generation and pass it over along with their own wisdom to the even younger generations. This type of passing down knowledge will lead to a better society in the future.

Wisdom is a gift that is granted from Allah (swt). He gives wisdom to whomever He wishes. However, it's important to remember that Allah (swt) has given every person a brain and intellect. And we are instructed to use them for the pleasure of Allah (swt) and in return we will be blessed by Allah (swt) and we will receive credits for it on the Day of Judgment. On that day, we will all be questioned about what we have done with our knowledge, our intellect, and our minds. Keeping that in mind, we should all prepare ourselves for our departure from this world to the Hereafter.

I. General

Most high schools, colleges and universities hold a Graduation ceremony at the end of the year for those students who finish their schooling programs. High Schools usually hold Prom, a formal dance, for the students typically held near the end of the academic year. Sometimes students get out of hand and indulge in alcohol and other things that are forbidden in Islam like, drugs, marijuana, sex and the like.

These distractions will prevent the graduating students from working hard to pursue higher education and/or getting a good job. As a result, they sometimes find themselves in trouble and/or becoming bad citizens. The following is an example of a speech that may be given at a graduation ceremony.

II. Speech

Ladies and Gentlemen, Brothers and Sisters

Assalamu `Alaikum

We are thankful and grateful to Allah (swt) first and foremost. Second, we wish to thank the administration, the faculty, the parents, the students and our guests. We are here today to share in the happiness of the graduating students. Now that you have come this far with your education, I know that you all will have very different plans and go in many different directions. Some of you may look to further your education, others may look for a job, and some of you may look for a spouse to get married. This is normal. We pray that you all find success and happiness irrespective of what route you choose.

The word Graduation means commencement; which means that the students are about to embark upon a new chapter in their life. In it, they should try to pursue more knowledge as was prescribed to us in Islam. Our beloved Prophet (pbuh) advised us seek knowledge from cradle to the grave. The more a person acquires knowledge, the more they will be humble.

Dear Friends

Here are some suggestions of how we, as Muslims, should celebrate the graduation of our children:

1. Special religious party in the Masjid
2. Go Camping for a week so the students can enjoy nature.
3. Have picnics for families to come together and socialize.
4. Visit different Masajid and learn more about each of them.
5. Visit a cemetery and teach them to make Du`aa' for the dead.
6. Travel to Makkah and Madina and make Umrah.
7. Start a school for recitation and memorization of Qur'an.
8. Take the students downtown to see how the homeless people live.

III. Final Remarks

Dear Brothers and Sisters

Graduating from a Secular Education program is not enough for our Muslim students. Muslim parents need to teach their children about Islam from Qur'an, Hadith, Seerah, Shari'ah, and so on. Therefore, a Muslim should be simultaneously learning their Islamic studies as well as their secular studies. Islam is a complete way of life and Muslims should learn first and then apply both Science/Technology and Religion to their daily life. Muslims should put into practice what they've learned and be thankful to Allah (swt), to parents, and to teachers for the knowledge they've acquired. Allah (swt) will bless you even more for being grateful to all those who have helped you learn. May Allah bless you all. Ameen!

I. Introduction

It is very exciting to know that Muslims all over the world encourage their children to memorize the whole Qur'an in its entirety. This is also the case with non-Arab speaking Muslims. Though the Qur'an was revealed in Arabic and is preserved in its original form in Arabic, many millions of Muslims around the world, young and old, have memorized the entire Qur'an despite their national origin.

The Qur'an is composed of a total of 114 chapters and more than 600 pages. The total number of Ayat (verses) in the Qur'an is 6, 236 and the total number of letters is 323, 671.

The Qur'an has been preserved by Allah (swt) since its revelation and will continue to be preserved until the Day of Judgment. For the last 14 centuries, the Qur'an was passed down from generation to generation by memorization. This is why we encourage our children to memorize the Qur'an in its entirety. It is important to reward your child for all their hard work and celebrate after they have completed memorizing the entire Qur'an. The parents should invite their relatives and friends as well as a Muslim scholar to say few words during the celebration.

It's important to know that an Aameen celebration is totally different from a Hifzul Qur'an celebration. An Aameen party is given when a child reads the whole Qur'an in its entirety for the first time; however, the child has not memorized it. A Hifzul Qur'an celebration is given once a child has read it and memorized the whole Qur'an. Once the child has completed its memorization, the child is known as a Haafiz.

II. Speech of the Speaker

Ladies and Gentlemen; Brothers and Sisters:

Assalamu `Alaikum

We thank Allah (swt) first and foremost for bringing us to this noble occasion. We are thankful to the family for inviting us and we thank you all for attending. We are here to share in the family's happiness and the one who has memorized the whole Qur'an.

I am sure that our new Haafiz who just finished memorizing the Qur'an is also very happy today because it took you an average of two complete years to complete. It is not an easy task but it is very rewarding. My advice to you is to read and recite as many verses and chapters that you can everyday; otherwise, you will forget what you memorized. Also try to understand the meaning of the verses you've memorized. Try to practice what you've learned and what you've understood. Teach others how to read Qur'an with its proper rules and regulations. Further, try to help others memorize the Qur'an. By reciting Qur'an in public to different groups of people and at different occasions, it will give you the reinforcement to preserve the Qur'an in your heart and brain.

III. Final Remarks

Ladies and Gentlemen; Brothers and Sisters:

The blessings for reading Qur'an go beyond our imagination. A knowledgeable person who knows how to read the Qur'an will get (10) ten blessings for each letter he reads. For those who are non-Arabic speakers and find it difficult to read Arabic, they will receive double the reward of an Arabic speaking person for every letter, i.e. Alif, Laam, Meem is composed of (3) three letters. You'll get (30) credits for the first letter, Alif, and you'll get (60) blessings for the second letter, etc. It's important to encourage each other to read the Qur'an and listen to its recitation daily. We pray to Allah (swt) to bless all of us who are here today. Ameen!

Chapter (50)	Aameen Celebration

I. Introduction

The Aameen party or celebration is given to honor the person, namely a child, who has finished reading the whole Qur'an with proper pronunciation. However, it does not necessarily mean that the child understood what they read nor does it mean that the child has memorized the Qur'an. It means that they have completed reading the whole Qur'an under the supervision of a teacher.

The speaker attending an Aameen party should use wisdom and know what to say to the audience as well as to the one who has finished reading the Qur'an. The following is a good source of information to share at such an occasion.

II. Speech

Dear Brothers and Sisters

Assalamu `Alaikum.

As you are aware, there are several different types of occasions in which Muslim families will gather to celebrate such as:

1. Waleemah
2. `Aqeeqah
3. Aameen
4. Hifzul Qur'an
5. Aayate Kareemah
6. Qur'an Khane, and
7. Many more

Today we are celebrating the Khatme-Qur'an also known as Aameen celebration. Allah (swt) encourages us to read Qur'an as well as listen to its recitation by other scholars.

1. Allah (swt) says the following in Surah Al-Nahl (The Bees) regarding reading the Qur'an:

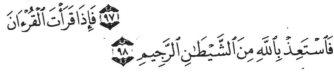

When you do read the Qur'an, seek Allah's protection from Satan, the Rejected One. (16:98)

2. Allah (swt) says the following in Surah Al-A'raaf (Heights) regarding listening to the recitation of the Qur'an:

When the Qur'an is read, listen to it with attention, and hold your peace: that you may receive Mercy. (7:204)

Dear Brothers and Sisters

Our beloved Prophet (pbuh) encouraged all of us to read the Qur'an so that we will receive blessings and credits from Allah (swt). Some of the rewards that we receive are as follows:

For every letter one reads from Qur'an, they will get ten (10) credits if they know how to read Arabic. However, if a person does not know how to read perfectly, they will get (20) credits for every letter. Our Prophet (pbuh) mentioned at that time that Alif-Laam-Meem is considered (3) letters. Therefore a person may get 30 or 60 credits just for reading those (3) letters. This is a great encouragement for the non-Arabic speaking Muslims to try and read as much as they can.

171

Dear Brothers and Sisters

As we are celebrating today the graduation of Khatme-Qur'an, it's important to note that a graduation is really a commencement; which means that the one who has finished reading the Qur'an must start all over again. However, this time, he/she should try to read better than the first time with all the rules and regulations. Further, he should try to understand the meaning of the verses that he is reading and memorize as many verses as possible. Lastly, he should practice what he has learned and teach others and deliver the message of the Qur'an to Muslims and non-Muslims.

III. Final Remarks

Dear Brothers and Sisters

We are grateful to Allah (swt) that we are here celebrating a good cause rather than being in Hollywood, watching TV, or doing something else that's meaningless. We are also thankful to the family who invited us here today. We pray for your happiness and the happiness of all of your relatives. We also pray for the happiness of all of you who attended this function today. May Allah (swt) bless you all reward you for being here.

For your information, the Angels are present here right now taking pictures of us and recording our gathering. This will count as a witness, a blessing, and a reward for you on the Day of Judgment. The following is the Du'aa that is recited after one completes reading the Qur'an. It is called Du`aa' Khatme Qur'an:

Du`aa' Khatme Qur'an

172

دُعَاءُ خَتْمِ الْقُرْآنِ

اللَّهُمَّ ارْحَمْنِي بِالْقُرْآنِ وَاجْعَلْهُ لِي إِمَامًا وَنُورًا وَهُدًى وَرَحْمَةً اللَّهُمَّ ذَكِّرْنِي مِنْهُ مَا نَسِيتُ وَعَلِّمْنِي مِنْهُ مَا جَهِلْتُ وَارْزُقْنِي تِلَاوَتَهُ آنَاءَ اللَّيْلِ وَأَطْرَافَ النَّهَارِ وَاجْعَلْهُ لِي حُجَّةً يَا رَبَّ الْعَالَمِينَ ✸ اللَّهُمَّ أَصْلِحْ لِي دِينِي الَّذِي هُوَ عِصْمَةُ أَمْرِي وَأَصْلِحْ لِي دُنْيَايَ الَّتِي فِيهَا مَعَاشِي وَأَصْلِحْ لِي آخِرَتِي الَّتِي فِيهَا مَعَادِي وَاجْعَلِ الْحَيَاةَ زِيَادَةً لِي فِي كُلِّ خَيْرٍ وَاجْعَلِ الْمَوْتَ رَاحَةً لِي مِنْ كُلِّ شَرٍّ ✸ اللَّهُمَّ اجْعَلْ خَيْرَ عُمُرِي آخِرَهُ وَخَيْرَ عَمَلِي خَوَاتِمَهُ وَخَيْرَ أَيَّامِي يَوْمَ أَلْقَاكَ فِيهِ ✸ اللَّهُمَّ إِنِّي أَسْأَلُكَ عِيشَةً هَنِيَّةً وَمِيتَةً سَوِيَّةً وَمَرَدًّا غَيْرَ مُخْزٍ وَلَا فَاضِحٍ ✸ اللَّهُمَّ إِنِّي أَسْأَلُكَ خَيْرَ الْمَسْأَلَةِ وَخَيْرَ الدُّعَاءِ وَخَيْرَ النَّجَاحِ وَخَيْرَ الْعِلْمِ وَخَيْرَ الْعَمَلِ وَخَيْرَ الثَّوَابِ وَخَيْرَ الْحَيَاةِ وَخَيْرَ الْمَمَاتِ وَثَبِّتْنِي وَثَقِّلْ مَوَازِينِي وَحَقِّقْ إِيمَانِي وَارْفَعْ دَرَجَتِي وَتَقَبَّلْ صَلَاتِي وَاغْفِرْ خَطِيئَاتِي

وَأَسْأَلُكَ الْعُلَا مِنَ الْجُنَّةِ ۞ اللَّهُمَّ إِنِّي أَسْأَلُكَ مُوجِبَاتِ رَحْمَتِكَ
وَعَزَائِمَ مَغْفِرَتِكَ وَالسَّلَامَةَ مِنْ كُلِّ إِثْمٍ وَالْغَنِيمَةَ مِنْ كُلِّ بِرٍّ
وَالْفَوْزَ بِالْجَنَّةِ وَالنَّجَاةَ مِنَ النَّارِ ۞ اللَّهُمَّ أَحْسِنْ عَاقِبَتَنَا فِي
الْأُمُورِ كُلِّهَا وَأَجِرْنَا مِنْ خِزْيِ الدُّنْيَا وَعَذَابِ الْآخِرَةِ ۞
اللَّهُمَّ اقْسِمْ لَنَا مِنْ خَشْيَتِكَ مَا تَحُولُ بِهِ بَيْنَنَا وَبَيْنَ مَعْصِيَتِكَ وَمِنْ
طَاعَتِكَ مَا تُبَلِّغُنَا بِهَا جَنَّتَكَ وَمِنَ الْيَقِينِ مَا تُهَوِّنُ بِهِ عَلَيْنَا
مَصَائِبَ الدُّنْيَا وَمَتِّعْنَا بِأَسْمَاعِنَا وَأَبْصَارِنَا وَقُوَّتِنَا مَا أَحْيَيْتَنَا
وَاجْعَلْهُ الْوَارِثَ مِنَّا وَاجْعَلْ ثَأْرَنَا عَلَى مَنْ ظَلَمَنَا وَانْصُرْنَا عَلَى مَنْ
عَادَانَا وَلَا تَجْعَلْ مُصِيبَتَنَا فِي دِينِنَا وَلَا تَجْعَلِ الدُّنْيَا أَكْبَرَ هَمِّنَا
وَلَا مَبْلَغَ عِلْمِنَا وَلَا تُسَلِّطْ عَلَيْنَا مَنْ لَا يَرْحَمُنَا ۞ اللَّهُمَّ لَا تَدَعْ لَنَا
ذَنْبًا إِلَّا غَفَرْتَهُ وَلَا هَمًّا إِلَّا فَرَّجْتَهُ وَلَا دَيْنًا إِلَّا قَضَيْتَهُ وَلَا حَاجَةً
مِنْ حَوَائِجِ الدُّنْيَا وَالْآخِرَةِ إِلَّا قَضَيْتَهَا يَا أَرْحَمَ الرَّاحِمِينَ ۞ رَبَّنَا
آتِنَا فِي الدُّنْيَا حَسَنَةً وَفِي الْآخِرَةِ حَسَنَةً وَقِنَا عَذَابَ النَّارِ
وَصَلَّى اللهُ عَلَى نَبِيِّنَا مُحَمَّدٍ وَعَلَى آلِهِ وَأَصْحَابِهِ
الْأَخْيَارِ وَسَلَّمَ تَسْلِيمًا كَثِيرًا

SUPPLICATION FOR RECITATION OF
THE WHOLE QUR'AN

In The Name of Allah, Most Beneficent, Most Merciful

Oh Allah! Have mercy on me, in the name of the Great Qur'an; make it an Imam and light for me, as well as guidance and mercy.

Oh Allah! Make me remember what I have forgotten of, and make me recite it in the hours of the night and the day; make it an argument for me, You are the Sustainer of (all) the worlds.

Oh Allah! Make my religion accurate for me, in which lies the infallibility of existence. Make good for me this world in which I shall spend my life in, and make good for me the hereafter to which I shall return. Make life an increase in every good thing for me. Make death a rest from every evil for me.

Oh Allah! Make the best part of my life to be the latter portion of it, and the best of my deeds their finishing and the best of my days is the day I meet You in the Day of Judgment.

Oh Allah! I ask You for a happy life, and an equitable death, a return with neither humiliation nor disgrace.

Oh Allah! I ask for the best that one can ask You for, and the best of supplication, the best success, the best deeds, the best reward, the best life, the best death, and strengthen me and increase the weight in the measure in my favor. Make true my faith and raise my ranking, accept my prayers, forgive my mistakes and I ask You a high level in heaven.

Oh Allah! I ask You for those which cause me to earn Your mercy and invite Your forgiveness, and the safety from every sin, the gain from every righteousness, the success of going to heaven, and the salvation from the fire.

Oh Allah! Make good our ending in all deeds, and prevent us from the humiliation of this world and the punishment of the hereafter.

Oh Allah! Give us the amount of fearing You which is enough to be a barrier between us and disobeying You, and enough obedience to let us reach Your heaven, enough certainty to ease on us the calamities of this world. Make us enjoy our hearing, our vision, and our strength as long as we live. Make them all to be what will be inherited to us (or what remains in our account). Make possible our revenge against those who did injustice to us. Give us victory on those who chose to be our enemies. Do not let our main misfortune be in our religion nor let the world be our main concern and the goal of our knowledge nor empower against us those who do not show us mercy.

Oh Allah! Do not let any of our sins go without forgiving it, nor any stress without relieving it, nor a debt without paying it, nor any need of the needs of this world and the hereafter without being faithful. Oh, You are the Most Merciful among those who have mercy.

Our Lord! Give us which is good in this world and which is good in the hereafter and guard us from the doom of fire. May Allah's (swt) mercy be upon our Prophet Muhammad (pbuh), his family, and his selected companions, and may He bless all of them with great blessings.

Chapter (51)　　Qur'an Khane　(Part 1)

I.　Introduction

Whenever there is a tragedy or a crisis that takes place in a family, the community members will offer their support the bereaved family and offer condolences whether it's sickness, death or natural disaster. In the case of a death, families usually gather at the mosque to read the whole Qur'an for the deceased. Each person tries to read one volume out of the thirty volumes of the whole Qur'an. After the entire Qur'an has been read by the community, the Imam will give a speech followed by a Du'aa' (supplication) for the deceased, and for all. Then food is served by the bereaved family on behalf of the deceased person.

This tradition is observed by many Muslims all over the world as well as in America. The ceremony of Qur'an Khane is usually held immediately after burial, and repeated three days later, one week later, and forty days after the burial. Of course, this ceremony should not be held during schools hours rather in the late afternoon or early evening.

If a student of an Islamic school unexpectedly passes away, the school must show sympathy to the bereaved family and make a public appearance during the burial. A representative of the school's administration in addition to the student's class should be present at the burial service in order to offer condolences to the family of the deceased student. Although this practice is not prescribed as part of the teachings of Islam, it has been widely practiced by Muslims all over the world and has become part of their customs and traditions. The following is an example of a speech that could be offered at such an occasion:

II.　Speech

Dear Brothers and Sisters

Assalamu `Alaikum

Innaa Lillahi Wa Innaa Ilayhi Raajioon

We are from Allah, and back to Allah we will return.

For the bereaved family, we offer our deepest condolences. This is a life of tests, and we will be tested. Everyone will be tested by Allah (swt) with what we like and other times with what they don't like. In this life, we are required to practice patience and Salat. In Surah Al-Baqarah (The Cow), Allah (swt) says:

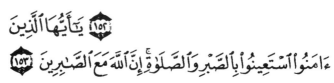

O you who believe! Seek help with patient Perseverance and prayer: for God is for those who patiently persevere. (2:153)

However, in Surah Al-`Imran, Allah (swt) says the following:

O you who believe! Persevere in patience and constancy; vie in such perseverance; strengthen each other; and fear Allah; that you may prosper. (3:200)

Dear Brothers and Sisters

Remember this! Whoever claims to be a faithful believer will be tested by Allah (swt). For this reason, in Surah Al-`Ankaboot (The Spider), Allah (swt) says:

178

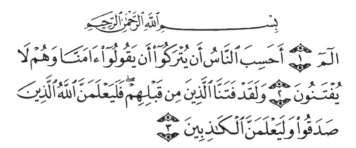

Alif. Lam. Mim. Do men think that they will be left alone on saying, "We believe", and that they will not be tested? We did test those before them, and Allah will certainly know those who are true from those who are false. (29:1-3)

My Dear Brothers and Sisters- we should do the following in hard times and in times of crisis?

1. One has to be patient.
2. One has to pray extra Salat.
3. One has to read and to listen to Qur'an.
4. One has to make charity (Sadaqah).
5. One has to make Du`aa' (Supplication).
6. One may invite friends to read Qur'an with them and make special Du`aa' (Supplication) for them.

III. Final Remarks

Dear Brothers/Sisters

It's important to remember that life on this planet earth is short and will be a life of testing by Allah (swt). Every person will be tested differently and in one way or another. We need to learn to be patient and submit to the will of Allah (swt) so that we will get credits and blessings from Him in our next life. We ask Allah (swt) to give patience, peace and blessings to the family who has been hurt through this crisis. May Allah (swt) bless you. Ameen!

And I would like to close with the following **Du`aa':**

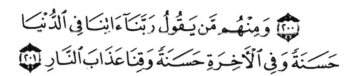

Our Lord! Grant us good in this world and good in the Hereafter, and save us from the chastisement of the fire (2:201)

Al-Fatiha or the Opening Chapter
In the Name of Allah,
Most Gracious Most Merciful

Chapter (52)   Qur'an Khane (Part 2)

I. Introduction

In this chapter, we'll discuss **Qur'an Khane** again however, its function here is totally different from that of the previous chapter. Many Muslims, upon buying a new home, or opening a new business, corporation, or clinic, will want to thank Allah (swt) and will ask for Him to bless them in their new purchase. In doing so, they'll invite friends and relatives to come to their new house or office building for a Qur'an Khane celebration. They request each one of their guests to read at least one volume from the Qur'an. They work together as a group to finish reading the whole Qur'an in an hour or so.   Afterwards, they'll ask the invited speaker to say few words and make Du`aa' so that Allah (swt) will bless them, their home, their clinic, or their business.

II. Speech

Dear Brothers and Sisters

Assalamu `Alaikum

Mabrook and Alf-Mabrook

This is an Arabic Expression which means blessings and one thousand blessings to come to you from Allah (swt) for the purchase of your new home, office, clinic or business.

We thank you for inviting us to join you and share in your happiness. We really enjoyed the company of good friends here today. Moreover, we really enjoyed the spirituality of reading the Qur'an and making Khatme Qur'an.

Dear Brothers and Sisters: Whoever of you has read from the Qur'an today has received blessings for yourself as well as for the host. For every letter you read, you received 10-20 blessings from Allah (swt) depending upon your reading level and knowledge of how to read Qur'an. Inviting friends to read Qur'an, listen to Qur'an, and to make special Du`aa' for the host to be blessed by Allah (swt) is an excellent way to celebrate this noble occasion. The more we are thankful to Allah (swt), the more we will be blessed in our lives either directly or indirectly.

Dear Brothers and Sisters

When we read the Qur'an as a group, it is important to complement one another and encourage each other to reflect upon the meanings of the verses. The following Ayat from the Qur'an will shed some light on this topic.

1. Reading and Understanding

The Qur'an was revealed and intended by Allah (swt) to be an easy book to read and understand by all people, irrespective of their intellectual level. This is one of the miracles of the Qur'an without any doubt. In this regard, the Qur'an states in Surah Al-Qamr (The Moon) the following:

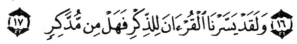

And We have indeed made the Qur'an easy to understand and remember: Then is there any that will receive admonition? (54:17)

2. Recitation of the Qur'an

When a believer wants to recite the Qur'an, they should seek refuge in Allah (swt) from the outcast of Satan. The Qur'an states in Surah An-Nahl (The Bees) the following:

182

When you do read the Qur'an, seek Allah's protection from Satan the Rejected One. (16:98)

3. Listening to Qur'an

When the Qur'an is being recited, the believing Muslims should listen carefully and have reverence for the word of Allah (swt). Qur'an states in Surah Al-A'raf (The Heights) the following:

When the Qur'an is read, listen to it with attention, and hold your peace: That you may receive Mercy. (7:204)

III. Final Remarks

Dear Brothers and Sisters

Let us make a special Du`aa'

- O Allah! Help us to live as honest and sincere Muslims
- O Allah! When we die help us to be faithful believers
- O Allah! Please bless the family who invited us, and bless their new house/ their office / their business
- O Allah! We all came here to give the host moral support and to pray for their happiness
- O Allah! Please give credits and blessings to all those who came here today. O Allah, this is Your gift to us.
- O Allah! Please accept our Du`aa'. Ameen!

Chapter (53)	Ayati Kareema

I. Introduction

In this chapter, we'll discuss an Ayah in the Qur'an called Ayati Kareema. This Ayah was recited by Prophet Yunus during a time of calamity and when he wanted to seek Allah's (swt) forgiveness for his sins. It is recommended that Muslims learn this Ayah and recite it at a time when a family or a society is afflicted with any tragedy such as sickness, earthquake, war, famine, flood, or any other distressful situation.

In times of sadness and distress, many Muslims will go to the Masjid and repeatedly recite Ayati Kareema as a group, followed by prayer and Du`aa' (supplication) so that Allah (swt) will bring peace and happiness to their lives and help them recover from whatever trial they may be facing. The Ayah, Ayati Kareema, is found in the Qur'an in chapter 21, which is Surah Al-Anbiyaa' (The Prophets). It is Ayah number 87 and it reads as follows:

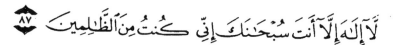

La Ilaha Illa Anta, Subhanaka Inee Kuntu Minaz Zaalimeen.

There is no one worthy of worship except You (Allah); and I am among those who transgressed my limits.' (21:87)

This Ayah was read by Prophet Yunus after he was engulfed in the belly of a whale. After reciting this Ayah, Allah (swt) saved him and ordered the whale to spit him out on the shore. Then Allah (swt) sent Prophet Yunus on a mission to a group of people whose men exceeded 100,000 in number. In Chapter 37 of the Qur'an, Surah Assaaffaat (Those Ranged in Ranks), Allah (swt) refers to the mission of Prophet Yunus as follows:

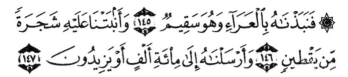

**But We cast him forth on the naked shore in a state
of sickness, and We caused to grow, over him, a
spreading plant of the Gourd kind, And We sent him (on
a mission) to a hundred thousand (men) or more.
(37:145-147)**

Traditionally, Muslims will gather and collectively recite
Ayati Kareema 125,000 times. They get together and each person
will recite the Ayah as many times as possible until the entire goal
has been reached. They use peas or beans to keep track of the total
number of times the Ayah has been read.

Once they are finished reciting Ayati Kareema for 125,000,
then the Imam will give a short talk followed by a Du`aa'. They
will offer one of the obligatory Salat and then finally the food will
be served.

This type of ritual observance does not require a vacation or a
holiday. Any individual who has been afflicted with a calamity
may organize such a service on his own. However, if a whole
society or an entire community or country has been afflicted with a
tragedy, then there is no objection if a local Masjid organizes such
a ritual for the benefit and participation of the Muslim community
who has been struck by a calamity.

It is important for the public school system to know about
these Islamic rituals and its significance just in case a Muslim
student needs to miss school on account of a tragic event that has
taken place either in the family or in the Islamic community. No
one can oblige the schools to do anything but it would be a good
idea if a teacher or the principal should mention it to the student
body.

II. Speech

Dear Brothers and Sisters:
Assalamu `Alaikum

Thank you for inviting us to this function. We are sorry to hear about this tragic situation. We ask Allah (swt) to grant peace, tranquility, and blessings to all those who are affected by this tragedy. I would like to remind you and remind myself that Allah (swt) asked us to be patient during times of crises. In Surah Al-Baqarah (The Cow), Allah says the following:

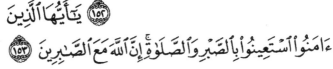

O you who believe! Seek help with patient perseverance and prayer: for Allah is with those who patiently persevere. (2:153)

We should all be grateful and thankful to Allah (swt) for allowing us to be invited to this function. May Allah (swt) bless all of you for accepting the invitation to share in the agony and distress of a friend or relative, family, community, or even with people overseas. If any one person makes a Du`aa' to Allah (swt) to relieve the distress of another person, the angels will say Ameen and the Angels will ask Allah (swt) to grant you the same as whatever you've asked for another. The following Du`aa' is a **Supplication for the Distressed:**

دُعَاءُ ٱلْكَرْبِ

ٱللَّهُمَّ إِنِّي أَعُوذُ بِكَ مِنَ ٱلْهَمِّ وَٱلْحَزَنِ، وَأَعُوذُ بِكَ مِنَ ٱلْعَجْزِ وَٱلْكَسَلِ. وَأَعُوذُ بِكَ مِنَ ٱلْجُبْنِ وَٱلْبُخْلِ، وَأَعُوذُ بِكَ مِنْ غَلَبَةِ ٱلدَّيْنِ وَقَهْرِ ٱلرِّجَالِ. ٱللَّهُمَّ ٱكْفِنِي بِحَلاَلِكَ عَنْ حَرَامِكَ، وَأَغْنِنِي بِفَضْلِكَ عَمَّنْ سِوَاكَ.

Allahuma inni A'uthu Bika minal hammni wal hazan; wa A'uthu Bika minal 'ajzi wal kassal; wa A'uthu Bika minal jubni wal bukhli; wa A'uthu Bika min ghalabatid daini wa qahrir rijali. Allahummak finee bi halalika 'an haramika; wa aghninee be Fadlika 'amman siwaka. Allahuma inni A'uthu Bika min 'Azabil qabri; wa A'uthu Bika min fitnatil mahya, wa fitnatil mamati. Allahuma inni A'uthu Bika minal ma'thami wal maghrami.

O Allah! (swt) I come under Your refuge from anxieties and grief; and betake Your refuge from impotence and inactiveness; and betake Your refuge from cowardice and niggardliness; and betake Your refuge from excessiveness of debt and oppression of people. O Allah! (swt) Suffice legitimate things for me, saving me from the illegitimate and make me independent in subsistence with Your grace from everyone except You. O Allah! (swt) I betake Your refuge from chastisement of the grave; and betake Your refuge from the seduction of anti-Christ from faith in You; and betake Your refuge from hardships of life and afflictions at the time of death. O Allah (swt)! I betake refuge from sins and debt.

We should all be patient and we should all accept what Allah (swt) ordains for us. The more patient we are, the more Allah (swt) will be pleased with us and the more He will bless us. The following Du`aa' may also be recited in times of difficulty:

- *Innaa Lillah Wa innaa Elaihi Raajioon*
  We are from Allah, and back to Allah we will return

- *La Howla Wa Laa Quwata Illaa Billaah*
  There is no might and no power except from Allah

- *Hasbunal Laah Wa Ni'mal Wakeel. Nimal Mowlaa Wa Ni'man Naseer*

  We are satisfied with Allah; the Best Guardian. Blessed with the supporter and Helper.

Let us read Surah Al-Fatiha (The Opening);

أَلْحَمْدُ لِلهِ رَبِّ الْعَلَمِينَ ۞ الرَّحْمَنِ
الرَّحِيمِ ۞ مَلِكِ يَوْمِ الدِّينِ ۞
إِيَّاكَ نَعْبُدُ وَ إِيَّاكَ نَسْتَعِينُ ۞
إِهْدِنَا الصِّرَاطَ الْمُسْتَقِيمَ ۞ صِرَاطَ
الَّذِينَ أَنْعَمْتَ عَلَيْهِمْ ۞ غَيْرِ
الْمَغْضُوبِ عَلَيْهِمْ وَ لَا الضَّالِّينَ ۞

In the name of Allah, Most Gracious, Most Merciful

Praise be to Allah The cherisher and sustainer of the worlds; Most Gracious; Most Merciful; Master of the Day of Judgment; You do we worship; And Your aid we seek. Show us the straight way; The way of those on whom You have bestowed Your Grace Those whose (portion) is not wrath And who go not astray. (1:1-7)

I. Introduction

Dear Muslims

Assalamu `Alaikum

My talk to you today is about "Good Friday". To a Muslim, Friday represents a holy and sacred day. It is a day where Muslims get together in the afternoon to congregate and offer the Friday Prayer together. In Surah Al-Jumua', Allah (swt) says

$$
\text{يَٰٓأَيُّهَا ٱلَّذِينَ ءَامَنُوٓا۟ إِذَا نُودِىَ لِلصَّلَوٰةِ مِن يَوْمِ ٱلْجُمُعَةِ فَٱسْعَوْا۟ إِلَىٰ ذِكْرِ ٱللَّهِ وَذَرُوا۟ ٱلْبَيْعَ ذَٰلِكُمْ خَيْرٌ لَّكُمْ إِن كُنتُمْ تَعْلَمُونَ ۝}
$$

O you who believe! When the call is proclaimed to prayer on Friday (The Day of Assembly), hasten earnestly to the Remembrance of Allah, and leave off business (and traffic): that is best for you if you but knew! (62:9)

As far as the Hadith is concerned, Prophet Muhammad (pbuh) informed us that Friday is the best day of the week for many reasons. In this regard, the Prophet said:

وَرَدَ أَنَّ يَوْمَ الْجُمْعَةِ خَيْرُ أَيَّامِ الأُسْبُوعِ : فَعَنْ أَبِي هُرَيْرَةَ رَضِيَ اللهُ عَنْهُ أَنَّ رَسُولَ اللهِ صَلَّى اللهُ عَلَيْهِ وَسَلَّمَ قَالَ : « خَيْرُ يَوْمٍ طَلَعَتْ فِيهِ الشَّمْسُ يَوْمُ الْجُمْعَةِ : فِيهِ خُلِقَ آدَمُ عَلَيْهِ السَّلامُ ، وَفِيهِ أُدْخِلَ الْجَنَّةَ وَفِيهِ أُخْرِجَ مِنْهَا . وَلاَ تَقُومُ السَّاعَةُ إِلاَّ فِي يَوْمِ الْجُمُعَةِ» رَوَاهُ مُسْلِمٌ وَأَبُو دَاوُد وَالنِّسَائِيّ وَالترمذي وصححه ،

Narrated by Abu Hurairah (May the blessings of Allah (swt) be upon him) that the Messenger of Allah (pbuh) said:

The best day the sun rises on is a Friday. Adam was born on Friday; He entered paradise on that day; He was taken away from it on that day, and the Day of Judgment will never occur except on Friday. Reported by Muslim and Abu Dawud

II. Friday vs. Jesus

Dear Muslims

According to Christian theology, they claim that Jesus, the Messiah, was crucified on a Friday and resurrected on a Sunday. This isn't true because Allah (swt) verified the truth about Jesus in Surah Al-Nisaa' (The Women), Chapter 4, verses 158 and 159.

Allah (swt) has informed us in the Qur'an that it was not Jesus that was crucified rather another person that looked like him. Islam considers the entire story of the crucifixion of Jesus as inaccurate. Islam teaches us that all people are born innocent and free of sin. No one person is responsible neither to purify another nor to die for our salvation. Allah (swt) did not appoint anyone to die for the sins of another. Therefore, Muslims do not accept that claim about Prophet Jesus and Muslims believe that he was a Prophet of God.

What we need to know is that no human being was born with an original sin. We were all born free of and absent of any sin. Adam did not and could not transmit any of his mistakes or sins to us. Adam and his wife made a mistake by eating from the fruit tree in paradise after God asked him not to. Adam immediately recognized his mistake and hence he and his wife Eve apologized and asked Allah (swt) to forgive them. Accordingly, Allah (swt) forgave them. Allah (swt) informed us in Surah Al-A'raf (The Heights) about their repentance. You may read about it in Chapter 7, Ayah number 24 in the Qur'an.

I would like to mention here that Jesus proclaimed himself to be a messenger and a servant of Allah (swt). Jesus did not and would not deny his being a servant and a slave of Allah (swt). You may read about this further in Surah Al-Nisaa' (The Women), Chapter (4:172).

III. More about Jesus

Dear Muslims

On the Day of Judgment, Allah (swt) will bring Jesus forth to stand in front of all of his followers. Jesus will be asked by God whether or not he informed people to worship him or his mother, the Virgin Mary. Jesus will say, "No, I did not and if I did, You (God) certainly would have known about it. Jesus persistently informed the people and his followers to worship Allah (swt) and Allah (swt) Alone. It was man who changed the Christian script and theology and thru this, many Christians have been led astray from God and the teachings of Jesus. On that Day, Jesus will submit himself completely to Allah (swt) and relinquish himself from any responsibility and any mistakes committed by his followers. You may read about this further in the Qur'an in Surah Al-Mai`dah (The Table Spread), Chapter (5:116-118).

Jesus performed his role as a Messenger of God and later Allah (swt) ended his life on earth and ascended him to the heavens away from the disbelievers. One may read about his assention in Surah Al-`Imran (The Family of Al-`Imran), Chapter (3:55)

The creation of and the death of Jesus was one of the miracles of Allah (swt). He was created miraculously from a mother but without a father. When his life ended on planet earth, he was taken out of the crowd without crucifixion. This was a miracle performed by Allah (swt), not Jesus, and it does not make him a divine person, or part of Allah (swt), The Creator. Anyone who thinks that Jesus was divine should ask themselves, what about Adam and Eve? They were created without a father or a mother. Does that make them divine or part of Allah too? Don't you think that the creation of Adam and Eve was much more difficult than the creation of Jesus? None of them claimed to be divine! So why does anyone consider Jesus to be divine when Adam and Eve have even a greater miraculous creation and nobody considers them to be divine?

IV. Final Remarks

Dear Muslims

For Muslims, the day of Friday is considered to be a holy and sacred day. On this day, Muslims are summoned together for the Friday Prayer to discuss some of the pertinent topics related to the Muslim Ummah.

Muslims are to remember Allah (swt) on Friday more than any other day of the week so that they are in the constant remembrance or Zikr of Allah (swt). Further, they should say the Salat and Salam unto the Prophet Muhammad (pbuh) at every Salat and Allah (swt) will bless us ten times over.

When informing others about the Islamic faith, please do not argue with anybody. Everybody has their own beliefs and we have to respect others beliefs. Allah (swt) advised Muslims only to inform them about the Truth that He (swt) revealed in the Qur'an. We should not argue nor fight with anybody and it is not our job to convert anyone. If anyone wishes to learn more about Islam, then we, as Muslims, should be eager to sit and share with them about what Allah (swt) has revealed in the Qur'an about Jesus.

We ask Allah (swt) to guide us to the straight path. Ameen!

Chapter (55)   Thanksgiving

I. Introduction

Dear Friends

Assalamu `Alaikum

Once it was said that, "In order to be able to thank God, you have to first be able to thank those people who have done favors for you". It is not possible for us to be grateful enough to The Creator for all of His blessings that He has bestowed upon us. So the least that we could do is thank all those people whom God sent to help us, guide us, teach us, and show us the best way. Our ancestors have done a marvelous job in building our societies. We are all the beneficiaries and inheritors of their personal sacrifices. They deserve to be thanked for all that they have done for us. We should be thankful and proud of their achievements and the institutions they've built and left behind for us to use. Their contributions and sacrifices are innumerable so therefore, we should be forever grateful to them and to God, the Almighty, the Creator, the Most Merciful, the Ever Merciful, the Most Forgiving, the Most Generous, and the source of everything good.

II. Celebration vs. Needy

While people are celebrating Thanksgiving in USA, there are millions of people in different parts of the world who don't have any food to eat, water to drink, clothes to put on, home to dwell in, or medication to take. In the USA, there are a large number of homeless people that sleep in the streets. A few years ago, I visited the nation's capital in Washington, DC and I could not believe my own eyes when I saw a large number of homeless people living and sleeping in the streets (during the snowy winter season) around the White House. Apparently, the economic system of Free-Enterprise and Capitalism is not working for all Americans, namely those who are disadvantaged; however, it seems to be working great for those who are rich and privileged.

III. A Helping Hand

During the Thanksgiving Holiday season, it is wonderful that a large number of Americans come together and reunite with their families and close friends in order to celebrate, give thanks and spend quality time together. Many individuals and organizations partake in initiatives to feed the hungry, shelter the homeless, and help those who are deprived, needy and less fortunate so that they don't feel excluded during the holidays. The problem with this is that these noble gestures and Thanksgiving only take place once a year. We hope that more people will take it upon themselves to be gracious and generous to others throughout the year in order to demonstrate their thanks and appreciation to God everyday by helping those who are needy and less fortunate.

IV. Thanks

Muslims are taught to thank Allah (swt) daily. During each prayer, Muslims recite Surah Al-Fatiha in every Ruku'a, which starts with the first verse that says, "Al-Hamdu Lillaahi Rabbil 'Aalameen". This phrase means Praise be to Allah (swt), the Lord of the whole universe. Muslims are supposed to show their gratitude to Allah (swt) daily because He created them as human beings, the supreme creatures on earth, as opposed to animals or some other creation of God. Allah (swt) subjugated the entire universe for human beings. He delegated humanity to be His vicegerents on earth. The Muslims are asked to represent Allah (swt) on this planet earth and act as Ambassadors on His behalf. Further, Allah (swt) asks us to be thankful to Him by being thankful to other people who have helped them. Allah (swt) will bless those who are thankful to others. Our beloved Prophet (pbuh) once said:

Anyone who does not give thanks to people is not grateful to Allah.

On the other hand, the Qur'an is very explicit concerning thanks and appreciations. In Surah Ibrahim, Allah (swt) says:

And remember! Your Lord caused to be declared (publicly): "if you are grateful, I will add more (favours) unto you; But if you show ingratitude, Truly My punishment is terrible indeed". (14:7)

However, in Surah An-Naml (The Ants) Allah (swt) says:

Said one who had knowledge of the Book: "I will bring it to you before ever your glance returns to you. Then when (Solomon) saw it placed firmly before him, He said: "This is by the grace of My Lord!- To test me whether I am Grateful or ungrateful! And if any is grateful, truly his gratitude is (a gain) for his own soul; but if any is ungrateful, truly My Lord is free from all Needs, Supreme in Honor!" (27:40)

195

Therefore, we should always be thankful to Allah (swt) and to all those who do favors for us.

V. Final Remarks

The concept of thanks should not be one of lip service, only to be mentioned by the tongue. Thanks or giving thanks should be shown in our deeds and by our actions. Our deeds, behaviors, attitudes, and manners should all reflect the concept of being grateful to Allah (swt), the Creator of the Universe. Muslims should be the pioneers in this world in assuming such a responsibility of showing gratitude to Allah (swt) and giving thanks to others. Muslims should carry this demeanor with them throughout their lives so as to be role models in the community for others to follow. We ask Allah (swt) to guide all of us to do good before we die. Ameen!

God (Allah) says the Truth

I. Introduction

Dear Brothers and Sisters

Assalamu `Alaikum

All human beings, at some point in their lives, are likely to get sick in one way or another. Today, a variety of new illnesses are arising in people that were not found in people who lived in previous generations. Some ailments are simple and easy to treat, while others may be more difficult to diagnose and treat. No one will ever understand Allah's (swt) wisdom behind sickness; who will be sick, for how long they'll be sick, and why Allah (swt) chose a particular individual to be sick. Further, no one knows how to treat and heal all illnesses, except God. Allah (swt) and Allah Alone is The Best of Healers. Whoever is sick should seek the help of doctors but know that it is Allah (swt) that is healing them with the help of the doctors. Muslim scholars should be called upon to teach us how to use the methods of spirituality during illness so that Allah (swt) will grant us a speedy recovery.

These days, Medical doctors in the USA and Europe will agree that 50% of healing is done through some type of spirituality. Further, they claim that 40% of healing is attributed to their family, their social life, and the friends around them. And lastly, 10% of healing comes from the medication drugs itself.

For those of you who become sick, please do not think that Allah (swt) is mad at you and is punishing you with an illness. Allah (swt) is giving you more credits and blessings through your sickness. He is testing you in order to raise your level and status in paradise so that you may have first class treatment. The greater your Iman is, the more you will be tested by Allah (swt). Remember, the people on earth who were tested most with a variety of different tests were the Prophets. Allah (swt) tested Prophet Ayoob with his patience and his health. He lost all of his 12 children in one year; every month, one child would die. After losing each child, he used to say, "Allah (swt) gives, Allah (swt) takes, and I am patient. I am requesting Allah (swt) to give me credits". Then he became sick with scabies and later became paralyzed and could not stand up on his feet. Nonetheless, he continued to be patient.

II. Methods of Healing

There are a series of methods that can be used for healing the sick. Spirituality is the best method. Allah (swt) prescribed the Qur'an as a healing to Prophet Muhammad (pbuh), and through the Qur'an, Allah (swt) will give healing. Allah (swt) says in Surah Al-Israa' (The Night Journey) the following:

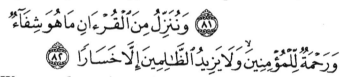

We sent down (stage by stage) in the Qur'an that which is a healing and a mercy to those who believe: To the unjust it causes nothing but loss after loss. (17:82)

The following is a list of things to do to recover from illness:

1. Read Ayatul Kursi and Surah Yaseen
2. Read the four (4) Qul A`oozu Surahs
3. Drink Zamzam Water
4. Make a special Salat before Fajr (Dawn)
5. Make extra Du`aa' (supplication)
6. Give charity (Sadaqah) to needy people
7. Listen to the recitation of the Qur'an more often
8. Visit different mosques and pray there
9. Make Jumu`ah salat at different Mosques

10. Socialize with different Muslim groups of people
11. Attend Halaqas and listen to lectures from many scholars
12. Go to Makkah and perform Umrah and/or Hajj. While there, drink Zamzam water as much as you can. Try to shower with Zamzam water. Make Du`aa' of Repentance and of Healing.
13. Ask others to make Du`aa' of healing for you.

III. Final Remark

At some or another, every human being will be tested with his health. Our life on this planet is a life of testings. When Allah (swt) tests someone, they should be thankful to Him so that they will receive credits and blessings from Allah (swt). They should exercise Sabr, patience, and perform Salat of Hajah. Allah (swt) says in Surah Al-Baqarah (the Cow) the following:

O you who believe! Seek help with patient Perseverance and prayer: for Allah is with those who patiently persevere. (2:153)

The following Du`aa' Shifaa' is for healing the sick:

١١٧٧ ـ وعن عائشة أن النبيَّ ، صلى الله عليه وسلّم كان يَعُودُ بَعْضَ أهْلِهِ يَمْسَحُ بِيَدِهِ الْيُمْنى ويقول : « اللّهُمَّ رَبَّ النَّاسِ ، أذْهِبِ الْبَأسَ (٢) ، واشْفِ ، أنْتَ الشَّافي لا شِفـاءَ إلاَّ شِفـاؤُكَ ، شِفـاءً لا يُغـادِرُ سَقَمـاً »

متفقٌ عليه .

O Allah! You are the Healer; there is no healing except through You and from You. Please! Give healing so that the sickness will go away. O Allah! Give healing to every sick person. Ameen! Praise be to Allah the Lord of the whole universe. Ameen!

Chapter (57)	Eulogy

I. Introduction

Dear Brothers and Sisters

Assalamu `Alaikum

On this sad occasion, there are no better words than the words of Allah (swt), in the Qur'an, and the sayings of His Prophet Muhammad (pbuh), in the Hadith. Allah (swt) told us that He will test each and every one of us and He instructed us to be patient and steadfast. In Surah Al-Baqarah (The Cow), Allah (swt) states:

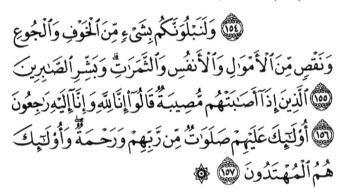

Be sure We shall test you with something of fear and hunger, some loss in goods or lives or the fruits (of your toil), but give Glad tidings to those who patiently persevere- Who say, when afflicted with calamity: "To Allah we belong, and to Him is our return"-

(2:155-157)

If you recite these three Ayat (155 – 157) from Surah Al-Baqarah, Allah (swt) will give you three types of rewards:

1. *Salawat;* prayers and blessings from Allah (swt)
2. *Rahmah;* mercy from Allah (swt)
3. *Hidayah;* guidance from Allah (swt)

II. Remembrance

Dear Friends

Remember folks, that Allah (swt) will give the maximum reward to those who are patient. In this regard, Allah (swt) says the following in Surah Al-Zumar (The Troops):

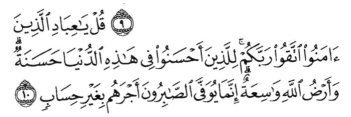

Say: "O you My servants who believe! Fear you Lord. Fear your Lord. Good is (the reward) for those who do good in this world. Spacious is Allah's earth! Those who patiently persevere will truly receive A reward with out measure!" (39:10)

Dear Friends

Allah (swt) asks the believers to be patient. He reminds us of our duty to perform the 5 daily prayers, which will help us to be patient and hold steadfast to the rope of Islam. In this regard, Allah (swt) says the following in Surah Al-Baqarah (The Cow):

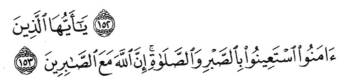

O you who believe! Seek help with patient perseverance and prayer: for Allah is with those who patiently persevere. (2:153)

Although today's occasion is sad, remember that, sooner or later, we are all going to die. This is part of life. When Prophet Muhammad (pbuh) died, it was a shock to his followers. In Surah Al-Zumar (The Troops), Allah (swt) addresses our beloved Prophet Muhammad (pbuh) and reminds him of the following:

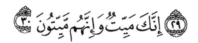

Truly you will die (one day), and truly they (too) will die (one day). (39:30)

During times of grief and calamity, we have to be patient. Our beloved Prophet Muhammad (pbuh) reminded us about the reward of those who are patient when they are hit with a crisis. He (pubh) said:

عن أبى هريرة رضى الله عنه أن رسول الله ـ صلى الله عليه وسلم قال : " يَقُولُ اللهُ تَعَالَى مَا لِعَبْدِيَ الْمُؤْمِنِ عِنْدِي جَزَاءٌ إِذَا قَبَضْتُ صَفِيَّهُ مِنْ أَهْلِ الدُّنْيَا ثُمَّ احْتَسَبَهُ إِلاَّ الْجَنَّــــــةَ "

رواه البخــــارى

It is narrated by Abu Hurairah (may Allah be pleased with him) that the Prophet (pbuh) said that Allah Almighty says that My believing creature has paradise when I take a loving member of his family, and he is patient. (Reported by Bukhari)

III. Final Remarks

Let's remind each other to be patient when Allah (swt) takes a loved one away from us. Remember earlier, I mentioned the three Ayat (155-157) from Surah Al-Baqarah. Let me request that we all recite these Ayat so that we may receive the multiple blessings of Allah (swt). I would also like to request that you make Du'aa' for the deceased person. May Allah (swt) bless you all and may Allah (swt) keep us on the straight path of Islam. Ameen! Let us ask Almighty Allah (swt) for forgiveness for our sins. And lets all make the following Du`aa' for our beloved deceased brother or sister.

Supplications for the Dead

Abu Hurairah reported God's Messenger (pbuh) as saying, "When you pray for the dead, make a sincere supplication for him". The following supplications have been taken directly from the sayings of Prophet Muhammad (pbuh) after being translated.

- **O Allah!** Forgive those of us who are living and those of us who are dead, those who are present and those who are absent, our young and our old, our males and our females.

- **O Allah!** Whomsoever of us You give life, keep him faithful to Islam while You give him life; and whomsoever of us You take in death, take him as a believer.

- **O Allah!** Do not withhold from us the reward of faith or to try us after his death.

- **O Allah!** So and so son/daughter of so and so is in Your protection and in Your nearer presence, so guard him/her from the trial in the grave and the punishment in hell.

- **O Allah!** Forgive him/her and show him/her mercy. You are the Forgiving and the Merciful One.

- **O Allah!** You are his/her Lord, You did create him/her. You did guide him/her to Islam. You have taken his/her soul, and You know best his/her inner nature and outer aspect. We have come asking forgiveness, so please forgive him/her.

- **O Allah!** Make him/her for us a righteous deed which has gone before us, a recompense gone ahead, a treasure and a reward.

- **O Allah!** Forgive him, have mercy upon him, give him peace and absolve him. Receive him with honor and make his grave spacious; wash him with water, snow and hail. Cleanse him from faults as You would cleanse a white garment from impurity. Requite him with an abode more excellent than his abode, with a family better than his family, and with a mate better than his mate. Admit him to the Paradise, and protect him from the torment of the grave and the torment of the fire. Ameen Ya Rabbal `Alameen!

Supplication for the Dead

دُعَـــاءٌ لِلْمَــيِّتِ

١٢٠٤ ـ وعن أبي هُريرةَ وأبي قَتادةَ ، وأبي إبْراهيمَ الأشْهَلي عَنْ أبيهِ ـ وأبُوه صَحابيٌّ ـ رضي الله عنهم ، عَنِ النبيِّ صلَّى الله عليهِ وسلَّم أنَّه صلَّى على جِنازةٍ فقال :« اللَّهُمَّ اغْفِرْ لِحَيِّنَا وَمَيِّتِنَا ، وَصَغِيرِنَا وَكَبِيرِنَا ، وَذَكَرِنَا وَأُنْثَانَا ،وَشاهِدِنَا وَغائبِنَا . اللَّهُمَّ مَنْ أحْيَيْتَهُ مِنَّا، فَأحْيِهِ عَلَى الإسْلامِ ،وَمَنْ تَوَفَّيْتَهُ مِنَّا، فَتَوَفَّهُ عَلَى الإيمانِ ؛ اللَّهُمَّ لاتَحْرِمْنا أجْرَهُ، وَلا تَفْتِنَّا بَعْدَهُ » (١) ، رواه الترمذي (٢) من روايةِ أبي هُرَيْرَةَ والأشْهَلِيِّ ،

Allahummagfhirli hayyina wa mayyitina, wa shahidina wa gha-ibina, wa sagheerina wa kabeerina, wa zakarina wa unthana. Allahumma man ahyaitahu minna fa ahyihi 'alal islam, wa man Tawaffaitahu minna Fatawaffahu 'alal imani; allahumma la tahrimna ajrahu, wala taftinna ba 'dahu.

Oh Allah! Forgive our living and our dead, and those of us who are present and those of us who are absent; and our little ones and full grown ones; and our men and our women. O Allah! Whom You keep alive from among us, keep him alive in Islam, and whom You cause to die from among us, make him die with faith (in You). O Allah, do not keep us away from his reward and do not put us in trial after him.

Verily, We have granted you a manifest victory. (48:1)

205

Chapter (58)   Visiting Prisoners

I. Introduction

When visiting a prison, it is important to be aware of your surroundings and know what to expect when you arrive. The following is a list of things to keep in mind when you visit the prison:

1. Many of the prisoners are African-Americans; some are Mexicans or Hispanics; and you may find some individuals who are Caucasians. Rarely will you find a Muslim from the Muslim part of the world in prison here in the USA.

2. Many prisoners will get locked up only to find Islam; many Americans accepted Islam while they were inside the jail.

3. After a person accepts Islam, they become very good citizens.

4. Most will adopt the best manners & behave with good morals.

5. They become devoted Muslims. They pray five times a day to include Salatul Jumu'ah in congregation. They fast the month of Ramadan. They refrain from eating pork, ham, bacon, lard, etc. They insist on eating Halal and Zabiha as well.

6. They enjoy reading Qur'an, Hadith and other Islamic literature. They are in need of more literature and some teachers to guide them. Reading by itself is not enough.

7. Some prisons may have a part time Da'iyah volunteer. Very few have a full time Imam. The US government doesn't really budget for Muslim chaplains; however, they have plenty of budgets for the non-Muslims chaplains.

8. In prison, other religious groups have the best privileges: i.e. Chapels, Chaplains, Bibles, Books and Literature, etc.....

9. The Muslims in prison don't have a place to hold or conduct religious services. They may have to pray in the chapel.

10. Some of those who accept Islam in prison may choose to follow the Nation of Islam, while others may choose to follow Imam W. D. Muhammad. Others may choose a different path or choose to be independent.

11. There are different types of prisons: County, State, Federal.

12. There are prisons for juveniles, youths, and adults.

13. There are prisons specifically for males & others for females.

14. Prisons may have different levels of security: min. and max.

15. You will not be able to enter a prison without being invited, scrutinized, identified, or being a bon-a-fide person.

II. Speech

Dear Brothers and Sisters: **Assalamu `Alaikum**

I am very thankful to you and to the Imam who invited us to visit and talk with you. I am very happy to be here with you today. You are not the first nor will you be the last to be incarcerated. Do not think of yourselves as criminals. It is possible that those who have put you in prison might have been wrong or the system might be wrong. Nonetheless, what's most important is that you have accepted Islam after being incarcerated. It is possible that if you stayed outside in the free world, you may have never had the chance to find and experience the beauty of Islam.

Remember what happened to our beloved Prophet Yusuf. He was an honest and sincere man. However, the system was wrong and those people who were controlling the system at that time were corrupt. Think about it, you are probably safer inside here than being out there. I will make special prayers (Du`aa') for you so that when you are released from here that you will make Da'wah and inform others about Islam. But while you are here, inform the others who are here with you about Islam because Im sure that they are looking for a better way of life and a better faith. If only one person is guided by Allah (swt) through your personality, character, behavior or manners, you will receive many credits and blessings from Allah (swt) from now until the Day of Judgment.

Your life on this planet earth is temporary and you will be tested by Allah (swt). At times, Allah (swt) will give us good things and blessings more than what we can make use of for the love of Allah and for the benefit of people around us. And other times, Allah (swt) may test us with something that is not good or may be harmful to us in order to test our patience and our obedience to Him. We should be patient, and we should make extra prayers and special Du`aa' (supplication). Remember that this life on planet earth is much shorter when compared to the life of the Hereafter. Similarly, the happiness we experience in this life cannot be compared to or equal to that of the happiness of Paradise in the Hereafter. The same thing can be said about the punishment, torture, and persecution that takes place on this planet cannot be compared to Hellfire of the Day of Judgment.

III.   Final Remarks

All of us will be tested on this planet earth in one way or another. Prison happens to be your test so try to make the best of it. Try to help each other in order to make a better life for you and for the people around you. I ask Allah (swt) to help us to be patient, to succeed in our trials and to grant us happy lives before we go back to Him. Again, I thank you for inviting me and may Allah (swt) bless us all. Ameen!

Chapter (59)   Protection From Shaitan

I.   Introduction

Dear Muslims

Assalamu `Alaikum

My talk is about Shaitan and how we can protect ourselves from them. Shaitan is sneaky, deceptive, and is an enemy to human beings. He tries his best to trap people into situations so that they will be in trouble with their Lord. If people are honest and sincere and they seek the truth from Allah (swt), they will not fall into the deceptive traps of the Shaitan. Even if Shaitan wispers to them and tries to get them in trouble, Allah (swt) will protect them from falling into his troubled network.

There are many Ayat in the Qur'an and a good number of Ahadith that speaks to how people can protect themselves from falling into the traps of Shaitan. In Surah Al-A`raaf (The Heights), Allah (swt) instructs us to seek refuge in Him whenever Shaitan tries to mislead you. The Qur'an states the following:

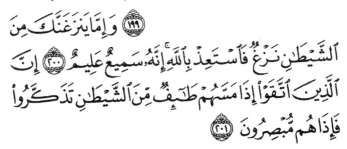

If a suggestion from Satan assails your (mind), seek refuge with Allah; for He hears and knows (All things). Those who fear Allah, when a thought of evil from Satan assaults them, bring Allah to remembrance, when lo! They see (aright)! (7:200-201)

II. Seeking Refuge

People should seek refuge in Allah (swt) on a daily basis by reading the last two Surahs from the Qur'an. They are Surah Al-Falaq (The Dawn) and Al-Naas (Mankind). They are called Al-Mu`awazatain, i.e. the two Surahs where people seek refuge in Allah (swt) from Satan, the outcasted one.

In Chapter number 113, Surah Al-Falaq (The Dawn), Allah (swt) says the following:

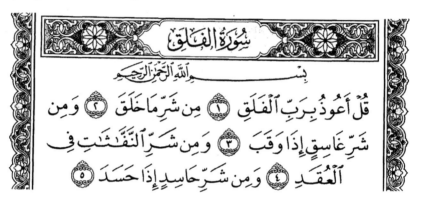

Say: I seek refuge with the Lord of the Dawn, From the mischief of created things; From the mischief of Darkness as it overspreads; From the mischief of those who blow on knots; And from the mischief of the envious one as he practices envy. (113:1-5)

Surah Al-Naas (Mankind) is the very last Surah in the Qur'an. The sequential number of this Surah is 114 and Allah (swt) says the following in this Surah:

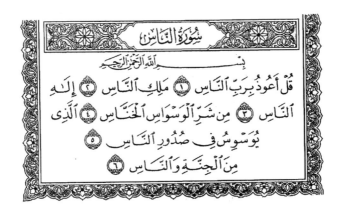

Say: I seek refuge with the Lord and Cherisher of Mankind, The King (or Ruler) of Mankind, The God (or Judge) of Mankind, From the mischief of the Whisperer (of Evil), who withdraws (after his whisper), (the same) who whispers into the hearts of mankind- among Jinns and among Men. (114:1-6)

Whenever Muslims read Qur'an, they are instructed by Allah (swt) to seek refuge with Him from the outcast Satan and, in so doing, Allah (swt) will protect them from Shaitan and Allah (swt) will allow them to have a better understanding of what they read and the meanings of the verses of the Qur'an. You may reference this in Surah Al-Nahl (The Bees), Chapter (16:98-100).

III. More Protection from Shaitan

In order to receive additional protection from Shaitan on a daily basis from morning until night, one needs to make a special Du`aa' that was prescribed by our beloved Prophet Muhammad (pbuh). The prescription is free, it works effectively, and it does not have any side effects. All it takes is a person's willingness to live in peace and harmony, someone who wants to live a happy life, and one who is committed to the prescription, i.e. the willingness to make use of it.

The following prescription was given to all of us so that we may be protected from Shaitan and his mischievous activities for the whole day. However, the prescription has to be used and practiced daily in order to be effective.

Whoever says:

La Ilaha Illa-Llah, Wahdahu La sharika lahu, Lahul Mulk wa Lahul Hamd, wa Huwa 'Alaa Kulli shay-inn Qadeer.

الحرز من الشـــيطان

« مَنْ قَالَ لا إِلَه إِلاَّ اللهَ ، وَحْدَهُ لا شَرِيـكَ لَهُ ، لَهُ الْمُلْكُ
ولَهُ الْحَمْدُ وهُو عَلَى كُلِّ شَيْءٍ قَدِيرٌ، في يَوْمٍ مائَةَ مَرَّةٍ كَانَتْ
لَه عِدْلَ عَشْرِ رِقَابٍ، وَكُتِبَتْ لَه مائَـةَ حَسَنَةٍ، ومُحيَتْ عَـنْه
مـائَةُ سَيِّئَةٍ، وكَانَتْ لَه حِرْزاً من الـشَّيْـطانِ يَوْمَهُ ذَلِكَ حَتَّى
يُمْسِى، وَلَمْ يَأْتِ أَحَـدٌ بَـأَفْضَلَ مِمَّا جَاءَ بَه إِلاَّ رَجُلٌ عَمِلَ
أَكْثَرَ مِنْه" . (رواه البخارى ومسلم عن أبى هريرة رضى الله عنه)

There is no one worthy of worship except Allah, the Only One; there is no partner with Him; He has the whole universe under His control; thanks are due to Him; and He has the power above everything.

By reading these words one hundred times daily, you will receive a reward from Allah (swt) equivalent to the freeing of ten captives; you will also get one hundred blessings, one hundred mistakes will be wiped out and off your record, and it will protect you from Shaitan for the entire day until night falls. No one will get a better reward except a person who did more than that.

IV. Final Remarks

In order to keep oneself protected from the Shaitan, one has to be in touch with and in constant communication with Allah (swt). At a minimum, we should be making our prayers, (5) five times a day and on time. Further, we should read from the Qur'an daily and listen to its recitation by other scholars. We should have our hearts attached to going to the Masjid, not only on Friday's for the congregational prayer, but as many times as possible during the week. We should be accustomed to making a series of Du`aa' for different occasions. We should keep our minds, tongues, and hearts active with the remembrance of Allah (swt). Let's pray and ask Allah (swt) to bless the Muslim Ummah all over the world. Ameen!

The Most Beautiful Names of Allah

Chapter (60)   You Are What You Eat

I.   Introduction

Dear Brothers and Sisters: **Assalamu `Alaikum**

The topic of my discussion today is a very interesting one. It is called <u>You Are What You Eat</u>. We will discuss the various factors that will impact our daily lives and have an affect on our personalities, character and behavior.

There are four main factors that affect and play a major role in molding the personalities, the character, and the behavior of each individual. They are the following:

1. Genetics and Heredity
2. The Foods You Eat
3. Environment and Society
4. Guidance from the Supreme Creator (Hidayah)

All these factors affect our beings in one way or another. The foods we eat affect us in all aspects of our lives; i.e. physical, physiological, biological, and mental, to include the shaping of our personality. In addition, the macro and micro environment plays a role in influencing the health of individuals as well. The following is a list of some factors that can affect eating behavioral patterns and can contribute to over-eating:

1. Ignorance
2. Poverty
3. Pleasure
4. Promotion
5. Compensation
6. Loneliness
7. Stress
8. Anxiety

While all these factors play a significant role in shaping who we are, there are things that we can do as Muslims to improve the quality of our personality, our character, and our behavior. We have to continually pray and ask Allah (swt) for guidance, forgiveness, blessings and mercy. We should read the Qur'an daily as well as listening to its recitation. We should strive to be humble in order to improve ourselves and to be close to the teachings of Allah (swt). All these ritual will have a positive affect on molding your character as a Muslim.

II. Health

Dear Muslims

The World Health Organization (WHO) of the United Nations (UN) defines Health as follows:

It is a state of complete mental, physical or social well-being, and not just the absence of disease.

The World Health Organization (WHO) approach did not include a spiritual component to its definition and factors that will affect the well being of an individual. The spiritual well being of an individual can affect one's physical entity either positively or negatively. It should be stated here that the factors affecting the health of individuals is a more comprehensive one as follows:

1. Food and Diet
2. Eating Habits
3. Diseases
4. Physical Activities
5. Spiritual Activities

In order to keep yourself happy, healthy and strong, you should examine the various types of food you are eating on a daily basis. You should eat less and work more; eat to live not live to eat. Allah (swt) revealed in the Qur'an a series of Ayat concerning health, tasty food and how to eat to live a healthy life.

Allah (swt) says in the Qur'an in Surah Al-Baqarah (The Cow) the following:

$$يَـٰٓأَيُّهَا ٱلنَّاسُ كُلُوا۟ مِمَّا فِى ٱلْأَرْضِ حَلَـٰلًا طَيِّبًا وَلَا تَتَّبِعُوا۟ خُطُوَٰتِ ٱلشَّيْطَـٰنِ إِنَّهُۥ لَكُمْ عَدُوٌّ مُّبِينٌ ١٦٨$$

O ye people! Eat of what is on earth, lawful and good. And do not follow the footsteps of the Evil One, For he is to you An avowed enemy. (2:168)

Furthermore, Allah (swt) prescribed for us to eat the best types of food. Allah (swt) says in Surah Al-A`raf:

$$كُلُوا۟ مِن طَيِّبَـٰتِ مَا رَزَقْنَـٰكُمْ$$

Eat of the good things We have provided for you. (7:160)

III. Final Remarks

It is imperative that you take care of your health before it is too late and you lose it. Be careful of **what** you eat, **when** you eat and **how much** you eat. The older you get, the less intake of food is required by your body and you should keep your body busy and working, not idle. The very best form of physical exercise is the performance of Salat. Every person should strive to perform extra prayers in addition to the required five daily prayers.

Always be cognizant of your health and remember You Are What You Eat. Please try your best to live a happy, healthy and strong life. Thank you for listening and may God bless you all. Ameen!

216

Chapter (61) Misconceptions About Halal Foods Part (1)

I. Introduction

Dear Brothers and Sisters
Assalamu `Alaikum

There are several misconceptions out there regarding Halal Foods. These misconceptions are primarily due to one's lack of knowledge of the Shariah on one side and the lack of scientific information on the other side. Furthermore, there is a scarce amount of information about practices and procedures of halal food that links early Islamic history to contemporary modern technology. In order to give real time information regarding Halal Foods, one must learn and recognize the various classifications and categories that foods may fall under; these categories extend from Halal all the way to Haram. The categories are as follow:

- Halal.....................lawful
- Mustahabb...............liked and recommended
- Maqbool.................accepted
- Jaa-iz....................permissible
- Mash-booh..............suspicious
- Makrooh.................not liked and not recommended
- Haram...................prohibited and unlawful

In addition to all of these classifications, there are several misconceptions out there about Halal food. It is very important to be mindful of the many misconceptions that exist about Halal foods among the Muslims. All of these Islamic classifications and misconceptions should be understood in order to ensure a healthy, wholesome, and Halal food diet. In this section, we'll list and discuss the many misconceptions out there and Insha Allah, in the next section, we'll explain them in detail. The following concepts are just a partial list of misconceptions regarding Halal foods:

Misconceptions:

1. Halal vs. Zabiha
2. Tahawwul vs. Istihaalah
3. Organic vs. Inorganic
4. Halal vs. Kosher
5. Unknown Slaughtering vs. Eat with Bismillah
6. Vinegar vs. Wine Vinegar
7. Apple Juice vs. Apple Cider
8. Olive Oil vs. Oil vs. Fats
9. NaNO2 vs. NaNO3 vs. Sodium Nitrite vs. Sodium Nitrate
10. Unknown: DES (hormone) ...Estrogen
11. Feeds: Meat, Blood, Vicera, Garbage

II. Specifics

Dear Muslims

By discussing these topics, it will be easier for Muslims to distinguish the differences and make better decisions regarding Halal Foods. However, if and when there is any question or doubt, one should call the company that produces and/or manufactures the food and verify the information. Another option would be to make inquiries to organizations and companies, such as Islamic Foods and Nutrition Council of America (IFANCA), who can disseminate information about questionable foods and ingredients and whether or not it is certified Halal or not. Further, Muslims may discuss these topics with Scholars who are scientifically and religiously qualified and informed to answer questions and disseminate information regarding Halal food.

It is incumbent upon every Muslim to seek knowledge and understand the foods we eat so as not to violate our religion by eating foods that are not permissible. It is not sufficient to seek guidance regarding Halal foods or the permissibility of a particular food with an Imam who is not aware or well informed about science and technology of manufactured foods in addition to the promotion of genetically engineered seeds and food products that will wind up in animal feeds by major companies in USA. The same thing could be said here; that it will not suffice to inquire about Halal foods with a scientist who has no knowledge of Shariah views and beliefs. In order to get accurate information, you'll need to ask someone who is qualified and has knowledge about Halal foods from a scientific standpoint and from a Shariah standpoint.

III. Final Remarks

We hope and pray that Muslim countries around the world will cooperate with knowledgeable and qualified institutions here in the US so that Halal foods can be known and certified all around the world. Ameen!

Chapter (62)   Misconceptions About Halal Foods
Part (2)

I.   Introduction

Dear Brothers and Sisters: **Assalamu `Alaikum**

In part (1), we discussed general issues concerning Halal Foods.   In this section, we will explain a few of those Misconceptions further in a little more detail.

1.   Halal vs. Zabiha

Any animal that is slaughtered correctly, according to Shariah, or incorrectly, by other practices, is considered Zabiha.   In order for animal to be considered Halal, it has to meet 3 requirements. First, the animal needs to be of a Halal source, such as chicken, cow, lamb, goat, sheep, camel or bird.   Second, the animal must be fed with plant like foods such as grasses, cereals, grains, seeds and other foods that do not contain any animal by-products. Otherwise, it will become Jallalah and not Halal.   Third, the animal should be slaughtered according to the Shariah (Islamic Jurisprudence) and Allah's name should be pronounced during the time of slaughter in order for it to be considered Halal.

2.   Tahawwul vs. Istihalah

Tahawwul means that a substance has changed into a different product through the process of hydrolysis such as when a starch turns into glucose; this is caused by a chemical reaction when the starch reacts with water to form glucose.   Another example of Tahawwul is when the substance fat is hydrolyzed and changes to become glycerol and free fatty acids.   These final product or compound is totally different than the original substance that we started with.   This is what is known as Tahawwul.

Istihalah, on the other hand, is the process of dissolving two liquids together, whereby it is not possible to separate or get back the original substance because it has already dissolved. For example, if alcohol is added to liquid or to water, then it is not possible to separate or catch the alcohol from the liquids because it has already dissolved with the liquid. This is known as Istihalah.

3. Organic vs. Inorganic

Many people are unaware of the definition or differences between both of these terms, Organic and Inorganic. Many companies try to encourage people to use organic products because it is either better or healthier.

What is important here is to understand the technical and scientific definitions of each. An organic compound is a chemical substance that contains carbon, nitrogen and oxygen (C, N, and O) elements all at the same time. I'd like to bring to your attention that urine and feces both contain C, N, and O at the same time, which makes them both organic compounds by definition; and no one would dare to eat those organic substances.

Inorganic compounds are those substances that do not contain all of these elements C, N, and O at the same time. Does this mean that we should not consume inorganic foods? That is another topic for discussion at another time but for now what important is to understand the definitions and differences between these terms.

II. Final Remarks

The most important lesson to take home today is to understand the definitions and distinctions between all of the terms we've discussed. I believe that by knowing them, we'll be equipped to make better decisions regarding the foods we chose to consume. I ask Allah (swt) help us to understand His truth the way He wants us to understand it. Ameen!

Chapter (63)   Misconceptions About Halal Foods
Part (3)

I. Introduction

Dear Muslims

Assalamu `Alaikum

Today we will continue discussing and contrasting some of the ideas related to the Misconceptions about Halal Foods. Previously, we've discussed Halal vs. Zabiha; Tahawwul vs. Istihalah; and Organic vs. Inorganic. Now I'd like to continue to discuss the remaining topics.

1. Kosher vs. Halal

Kosher foods are determined and labeled by whatever the Union of Rabbi decides to be kosher. Foods labeled Kosher may not necessarily mean that they are Halal for Muslims to consume. The way they bless the animal, the methods of slaughtering and the feeds given to the animals should all be known to Muslims before determining its permissibility. For example, Gelatin, which is sourced from a pig, is considered Kosher for the people of the Jewish faith. Their justification for this comes from the Food and Drug Administration (FDA) who says that the sequential Amino Acids of gelatin from pigs are similar to the gelatin that comes from plants. Therefore, the Union of Rabbi labeled pig gelatin as kosher. Muslims are prohibited from consuming pig gelatin. This is a good example of how something Kosher is not Halal and is actually Haram for Muslims to consume.

2. Unknown slaughtering vs. Eating with Bismillah.

During the time of the Prophet, it was alright to pronounce Allah's (swt) name on the meat of an animal and eat it even when the source of slaughtering or the person who slaughtered it was unknown. During that time, the meat of the People of the Book

(Christians and Jews) was permissible to eat by Muslims because in those days, the animals were fed a healthy plant diet with plenty of grasses, cereals, and other grains. Nowadays, animals are being fed meats, blood, viscera; in addition to being given hormones for accelerated growth and other unnatural remedies. This method of raising animals is not lawful according to Islamic law and therefore, constitutes the animals of today to become Jallalah, which means it is no longer Halal. Furthermore, the method of slaughtering used to be done by hand which is not the case today. Nowadays many slaughter houses will hit the animals with an electrical device which will shock the animals before they are slaughtered.   As a result, the animal looses consciousness and some may die before being slaughtered.

Islam demands that the animal should be Halal, the foods should be from grasses and plants. No animal sources and no hormones to be given to the animals. The method of slaughtering should be kind and gentle. It should be done in the Name of Allah.

3. Apple Juice vs. Apple Cider

This is a very common misconception whereby people think that both Apple Juice and Apple Cider are Halal to consume because they are sourced from apples. This is not true; apple juice is halal but apple cider is not. It is true that their main source is apple; however, each goes through a different fermentation process while extracting the juice from apple. Apple juice is sterilized and in doing so, the bacteria are destroyed and no alcohol is produced during fermentation.

On the other hand, Apple Cider is not sterilized so the bacteria are not destroyed and therefore, it produces an alcohol, Ethyl Alcohol to be specific, in the juice. Therefore, the presence of alcohol in the juice makes Apple Cider not Halal. We encourage you to drink apple juice but not apple cider.

II. Final Remarks

It is extremely important to understand what you are putting into your body; the types of food, where did they come from, and in the case of animals, how were they raised and how were they slaughtered. In recent years, we've seen many diseases, such as Mad Cow Disease and Swine Flu, develop in animals as a result of inappropriate feeding and raising methods. Unfortunately, the practices of caring for and feeding animals are not the same today as they were in the past. Therefore, the animals that were lawful and acceptable for Muslims to eat during the time of the Prophet (pbuh) are not lawful today due to the contemporary practices of raising animals.

We ask Allah (swt) to guide us to His truth. And we ask Allah (swt) to keep us from straying from His truth. Ameen!

Pillars of Iman
The Belief In:
Allah   Books   Hereafter
Angels   Messengers   Destiny

| Chapter (64)   Comprehensive Love |

I. Introduction

In an attempt to promote love, the Western Societies have introduced a holiday into the society called Valentine's Day. It occurs once a year, on February 14th of each year, and it's a highly commercialized holiday, boosting the economy with millions of dollars in revenues to corporations. The love that is promoted is based mainly on sex-relations. It is the type of love fit for a boy-friend and girl-friend relationship. Cards, flowers and gifts are exchanged that day and some people may be under the illusion that such a celebration will improve their relationship for the entire year to come.

This type of superficial love is only temporary and does not last. As Muslims, we should strive to establish an Eternal Love or a Comprehensive Love in our lives; otherwise the relationship may be destroyed and hate will be the end result of this so called loving relationship.

II. Types of Love

Dear Muslims   **Assalamu `Alaikum**

The following is an all inclusive list of different types of love which contribute to the love and success of any relationship. This is what is known as Comprehensive Love. This love includes:

1. Love of Allah and His Messenger, Prophet Muhammad
2. Love and respect of parents
3. Love and respect of the 'Ulama', i.e. the Muslim scholars, the knowledgeable people in Islamic Shari`ah, and the religious leaders.
4. Love and respect of the elderly
5. Love and respect to one another

III. Love of Allah

All types of love stem from the number one, main source of
love and that's Allah (swt). Hence, there cannot be true love on
this planet unless we believe in Allah (swt), love Him, obey Him,
and respect and obey His orders. Allah (swt) tells us in the Qur'an
that He will destroy those people who don't have such love and He
will replace them with a new generation of people who will love
Him and obey Him. In Surah Al-Ma'idah (Table Spread), Allah
(swt) says the following:

يَـٰٓأَيُّهَا
ٱلَّذِينَ ءَامَنُواْ مَن يَرْتَدَّ مِنكُمْ عَن دِينِهِ فَسَوْفَ يَأْتِى ٱللَّهُ بِقَوْمٍ يُحِبُّهُمْ
وَيُحِبُّونَهُۥٓ أَذِلَّةٍ عَلَى ٱلْمُؤْمِنِينَ أَعِزَّةٍ عَلَى ٱلْكَـٰفِرِينَ يُجَـٰهِدُونَ فِى
سَبِيلِ ٱللَّهِ وَلَا يَخَافُونَ لَوْمَةَ لَآئِمٍ ذَٰلِكَ فَضْلُ ٱللَّهِ يُؤْتِيهِ مَن يَشَآءُ
وَٱللَّهُ وَٰسِعٌ عَلِيمٌ ﴿٥٤﴾

***...Soon will Allah produce a people whom He will
love as they will love Him,... (5:54)***

The love of Allah (swt) necessitates our obedience to Him. A
Muslim makes a pledge of allegiance and offers obedience to Allah
(swt) on a daily basis. Our loyalty is foremost to Allah (swt)
before it is to any flag or any country. There is an Ayah in the
Qur'an that explains the total pledge of allegiance to Allah (swt) in
a beautiful way. This Ayah is found in Surah Al-An'am (The
Cattles) and Allah (swt) says the following:

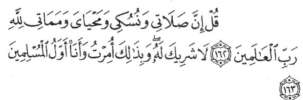

قُلْ إِنَّ صَلَاتِى وَنُسُكِى وَمَحْيَاىَ وَمَمَاتِى لِلَّهِ
رَبِّ ٱلْعَـٰلَمِينَ ﴿١٦٢﴾ لَا شَرِيكَ لَهُۥ وَبِذَٰلِكَ أُمِرْتُ وَأَنَا۠ أَوَّلُ ٱلْمُسْلِمِينَ
﴿١٦٣﴾

Say: "Truly, my prayer and my service of sacrifice, my life and my death , are all for Allah, the Cherisher of the Worlds: No partner has He: this am I commanded, and I am the first of those who submit to His will. (6:162-163).

IV. Love of Prophets

The love of Allah (swt) demands for us to love all of the prophets, especially Prophet Muhammad (pbuh). He is the final Prophet and the Final messenger of Allah (swt) to all mankind and to all other creatures in the universe. The Prophet said:

$$\text{لَا يُؤْمِنُ أَحَدُكُمْ حَتَّى يَكُونَ اللَّهُ وَرَسُولُهُ أَحَبَّ إِلَيْهِ مِمَّا سِوَاهُمَا}$$

No one will be a believer till the love of Allah and His Messenger is above the love of anyone else.
Narrated by Abu Hurairah

Our love to Prophet Muhammad (pbuh) necessitates our obedience to him and requires us to learn about and follow his teachings, his Hadith and his Sunnah. Allah (pbuh) demanded that we obey our beloved Prophet (pbuh) in order to earn the love of Allah (swt). In Surah Al-Imran (The Family of Imran), Allah (swt) says the following:

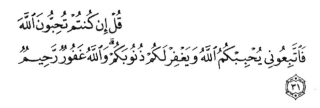

Say: "If you do love Allah, follow me: Allah will love you and forgive you your sins; for Allah is Oft-forgiving, Most Merciful. (3:31)

In the same Surah, Allah (swt) says the following:

قُلْ أَطِيعُواْ ٱللَّهَ وَٱلرَّسُولَ فَإِن تَوَلَّوْاْ فَإِنَّ ٱللَّهَ لَا يُحِبُّ
ٱلْكَٰفِرِينَ ﴿٣٢﴾

Say: "Obey Allah and His Messenger": But if they turn back, Allah loveth not those who reject Faith. (3:32)

V. Love of Parents

The love and obedience to Allah (swt) and His Messenger (pbuh) leads us to the love and respect our parents. Allah (swt) tells us in the Qur'an to love, respect and obey our parents as long as they are obedient to Allah (swt). In Surah Al-Isra' (Night Ascension), Allah (swt) says the following:

۞ وَقَضَىٰ رَبُّكَ أَلَّا تَعْبُدُوٓاْ إِلَّآ إِيَّاهُ وَبِٱلْوَٰلِدَيْنِ إِحْسَٰنًا إِمَّا
يَبْلُغَنَّ عِندَكَ ٱلْكِبَرَ أَحَدُهُمَآ أَوْ كِلَاهُمَا فَلَا تَقُل لَّهُمَآ
أُفٍّ وَلَا تَنْهَرْهُمَا وَقُل لَّهُمَا قَوْلًا كَرِيمًا ﴿٢٣﴾

Your Lord had decreed that you worship none but Him, and that you be kind to parents. Whether one or both of them attain old age in this life, Say not to them a word of contempt, nor repel them, but address them In terms of honor. (17:23)

There are many more Ayahs in the Qur'an and Hadith that you may read about pertaining to the subject of kindness to parents.

VI. Love of Scholars

The teachings of Islam demand from us to love and respect the Muslim 'Ulama,' the religious teachers, the Muslim scholars, and all those who have the knowledge of Islamic Shari`ah. It should be stated here that the Muslim 'Ulama' are the inheritors of the prophets.

Any group of people, who does not respect the Muslim 'Ulama', does not deserve to live on this planet earth. In a Hadith, the Prophet (pbuh) said that the death of one single 'Alim is equivalent to the death of one single nation. The revival of Islam is mainly through the efforts of the 'Ulama.' A good number of them had to suffer through torture, persecution and oppression by tyrant dictators in different parts of the world in order to deliver the message of Islam. The greatest jihad in Islam is to speak the truth in front of a tyrant leader as is stated in the Hadith of the Prophet (pbuh).

VII. Love of Elders and Love of others

We should also respect and love the elders as well as each other. No one Muslim can claim to be a believer until and unless you love for others what you love for yourself. The stability of any community cannot be established unless the members love and respect one another. Allah (swt), in the Qur'an, has already set forth the foundation for the believers and that is that they are brothers to one another. Allah (swt) says in Surah Al-Hujurat (Inner Apartments) the following:

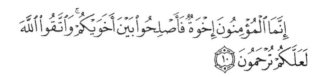

The Believers are but a single Brotherhood: so make peace and reconciliation between your two (contending) brothers; and fear Allah, that you may receive Mercy (49:10)

VIII. Final Remarks

Comprehensive Love is about having a true and sincere type of love to all those who deserve and have rights to your love, starting with Allah (swt). Allah (swt) loves those who love Him. It is important to know and identify Comprehensive Love so that you can teach and incorporate it in to your own families so that your relationships will be wholesome and complete. The following is a list of the groups of individuals whom Allah (swt) loves most:

1. Allah loves the beneficent...........................(Muhsinoon)
2. Allah loves the God-fearing .... (Muttaqoon)
3. Allah loves the equitable........................... (Muqsitoon)
4. Allah loves the steadfast........................... (Saabiroon)
5. Allah loves the purifiers....................... (Mutatahhiroon)
6. Allah loves those who trust Him ....(Mutawakkiloon)

On the contrary, I'd like to present a list of the groups of individuals whom Allah (swt) does not like. They are:

1. The disbelievers .... (Kafiroon)
2. The transgressors .... (Mu'tadoon)
3. The Mischievous .... (Mufsidoon)
4. The wrong-doers.................................... (Zaalimoon)
5. The Extravagant .... (Musrifoon)
6. The treacherous .... (Kha-inoon)
7. The arrogant .... (Mutakkabiroon)

Dear respected believers:

We ask Allah (swt) to guide us to the Siratul Mustaqeem (The Straight Path). We beseech His help, His mercy, His blessings and His forgiveness.

Let us ask Allah (swt) for forgiveness, and let us all raise our hands to Allah (swt) and make the following Du`aa':

اَللّهُمَّ أَعِنَّا عَلَى ذِكْرِكَ وَشُكْرِكَ وَحُسْنِ عِبَادَتِكَ ، وَأَصْلِحْ لَنَا دِينَنَا الَّذِي هُوَ عِصْمَةُ أَمْرِنَا ، وَآخِرَتِنَا الَّتِي هِيَ مَعَادُنَا ، وَدُنْيَانَا الَّتِي هِيَ مَعَاشُنَا ، وَاجْعَلِ الْحَيَاةَ زِيَادَةً لَنَا مِنْ كُلِّ خَيْرٍ ، وَالْمَوْتَ رَاحَةً لَنَا مِنْ كُلِّ شَرٍّ ، وَأَعِنْ وُلَاةَ أُمُورِنَا عَلَى مَا فِيهِ خَيْرُ الْإِسْلَامِ وَالْمُسْلِمِينَ ، وَاغْفِرْ لَنَا وَلِجَمِيعِ الْمُسْلِمِينَ ، إِنَّكَ نِعْمَ الْمَوْلَى وَنِعْمَ النَّصِيرُ .

* * *

231

Knowledge

Islam emphasizes the importance of knowledge to all mankind. It is only through true knowledge that one can appreciate the Creator of the Universe namely Allah (swt). Muslims are ordained to seek knowledge from cradle to grave and as far as a person can to obtain it.

In as much as seeking knowledge is a must for every Muslims, dissemination of knowledge is also incumbent on Muslims to the members of the society. The methods of disseminating the information should be lawful, as well as the truth is to be released to everyone. Hiding or keeping the true knowledge away from those who seek it, is considered a sin.

The best investment for every human being is through: perpetual charity (Sadaqa Jariya), useful knowledge that people shall benefit from, and a loving child who shall make special prayers for his/her parents.

Legality

The Foundation has been established and registered with the Secretary of the State of Illinois since January 8, 1987 as a non-profit, charitable, educational, religious and /or scientific society within the meaning of section 501 (c) (3) of the Internal Revenue Code.

The Foundation has a tax-exempt status with the IRS, and donations are considered tax-deductible.

Finances

The finances of the FOUNDATION are mainly from donations and contributions in the form of cash, assets and wills.

Inumerent Of Income

No part of the net earnings of the Corporation shall inure to the benefit of, or be distributed to, its members, directors, officers or other private persons except that the Corporation shall be authorized and empowered to pay reasonable compensation for services rendered.

Purposes

The purposes of the FOUNDATION are summarized as follows:

1. To promote Islamic Knowledge through education.
2. To create a better understanding of Islam among Muslims and non-Muslims through education and communication.
3. To publish books and other literature about Islam and its teachings
4. To disseminate Islamic Knowledge and education through TV, Radio, Video, and other means of mass communications.
5. To establish ecumenically among the religious people of America so that a better understanding will be created.

Activities

The activities of the FOUNDATION shall include, but not be limited to the following:

1. Publishing literature pertaining to Islam.
2. Producing audio cassettes and audio-visual tapes on certain topics of Islam.
3. Giving lectures related to Islam as a religion, culture and civilization.
4. Cooperation with other societies, foundations and organizations whose aims and objectives are similar to the FOUNDATION.

Knowledge In The Qur'an

The word knowledge ('ILM) is mentioned in the Qur'an more than 700 times in 87 different forms. Some of the pertinent Ayat are listed below.

1. The first Ayat revealed to Prophet Muhammad (pbuh) at Cave Hira' are in Surah Al-Alaq (The Clot) (96:1-5). They are related to knowledge of embryology through scientific investigation.

2. Allah honors all those who are knowledgeable. These people cannot be compared with the ignorant ones. See Surah Al-Zumar (The Troops) (39:29)

3. Only the knowledgeable people are those who appreciate the creations of Allah (swt). They are the ones who respect Him and worship Him with knowledge and humility. Please read Surah Fatir (The Creator) (35:28)

   Knowledge is in the Hands of Allah and it is at His disposal. People are to seek the true knowledge from its source namely Allah. Read Surah Al-Mulk (The Sovereignty) (67:26).

4. People are to seek knowledge from Allah (swt) and are to request Him to enrich them daily with 'ILM. Read Surah Taha (20:114).

Knowledge In The Hadith

Prophet Muhammad (pbuh) emphasized 'ILM tremendously and encouraged Muslims to seek knowledge in any part of the world. The following is a summary:

1. In one Hadith the Prophet says: "The Knowledgeable people ('Ulama) are the inheritors to the Prophets."

2. In another Hadith He encouraged Muslims to seek knowledge, saying: "Seeking knowledge is a must on every Muslim."

3. In another place, He demanded that knowledge is to be sought throughout lifetime, saying: "Seek knowledge from cradle to grave."

4. Knowledge is to be disseminated to all, and the best knowledge is that of the Qur'an, saying: "The best amongst you are the ones who learn Qur'an and teach it to others."

5. Knowledge is to be taught and to be carried on even after death. In His Hadith the Prophet said: "When a person dies, his deeds are over, except from three things; perpetual charity, a useful knowledge, or a good child who makes supplications for him."

The FOUNDATION will continue, with the help of Almighty God (Allah), to publish more useful literature.

Publications

I. Books On Health, Food And Nutrition:

1. Dietary Regulations & Food Habits Of Muslims
2. Overeating And Behavior
3. Islam On Alcohol
4. Alcohol In Beverages, Drugs, Foods And Vitamins
5. Cheese
6. AFTO and FAO
7. Food and Overpopulation
8. Honey: Food and a Medicine
* 9. Gelatin
* 10. A Muslim Guide to Food Ingredients
* 11. Understanding Halal Foods: Fallacies and Facts
* 12. Book of Healing
13. Shortening in Foods
14. A Manual on Food Shortenings
15. Food Supplementation
16. World Health Organization for Muslim Nations
17. Natural Therapeutics of Medicine On Islam (Co-authored)
18. Islamic Dietary Laws & Practices (co-authored)
19. Food and Nutrition Manual (co-authored)
20. A Handbook of Muslim Foods
21. Pork: Possible Reasons for Its Prohibition

II. Books About Friday Khutab:

* 1. Book of Al-Khutab
* 2. Islamic Orations
* 3. Orations from the Pulpit
* 4. Chronicle of Khutab
* 5. Friday Khutab

* 6. Khutab Al-Masjid
* 7. Khutab from Mihrab
* 8. Farewell Khutbah of the Prophet – Its Universal Values
* 9. A Manual of Friday Khutab

III. General Subjects:

* 1. Islamic Fundamentalism (co-authored)
* 2. Prostration – Sujood (new edition)
* 3. Understanding Islam and Muslims (Revised Edition)
* 4. Guidelines of Employment by Muslim Communities (co-authored)
* 5. Muslims and Non-Muslims: Face To Face
* 6. The Golden Book of Islamic Lists
* 7. Islam and Muslims: Myth or Reality
* 8. Islamic Awareness
* 9. A Course on Islamic Shari'ah
* 10. Da'wah Through Dialogue
* 11. Pillars of Islam
* 12. Life, Death and the Life After
* 13. Death and Dying
* 14. Book of Inquiries Vol. I
* 15. Book of Inquiries Vol. II
* 16. Family Values in Islam
* 17. Matrimonial Education in Islam (New Edition)
* 18. The Adolescent Life
* 19. Social Services and Counseling
* 20. Feasts, Festivities and Holidays
* 21. Understanding The Qur'an
* 22. Themes of The Qur'an
* 23. Book of Knowledge

* 24. Reflections from A Flying Falcon
* 25. Book of Wisdom
* 26. Book of Du`aa'
* 27. About Prophet Muhammad (pbuh)
* 28. Book of Hajj and Umrah
* 29. A Lifetime Journey
* 30. Most Beautiful Names of Allah Vol. (1)
* 31. Most Beautiful Names of Allah Vol. (2)
* 32. Book of Targheeb
* 33. Arabic Expressions, Listings and Glossary
* 34. Prepare Yourself and Speak

IV. Pamphlets:

* 1. Introducing Islam
* 2. Non-Muslims Through Muslim History
* 3. What Islam Says About ----
* 4. Living Together
* 5. What They Say About ----
  Prophet Muhammad (pbuh)

V. DVD's

- **Friday Khutbah Volume 1-3**
- **Variety of Salaat (Prayers)**
- **Fasting**

    * These publications are available from:

Foundation for Islamic Knowledge
P.O. Box 665
Lombard, IL 60148
Phone: (630) 495-4817 / Fax: (630) 627-8894
e-mail: drahmadsakr@hotmail.com website: www.ahmadsakr.com

Books To Be Published

1. They Left … We Follow
2. Guidance From Confusion – Accepting Islam
3. Book of Memories
4. Khutab of the Prophet
5. Khutab of Sacred Ahadith
6. Book of Khutab: Halal and Haram Foods
7. Welcome to the World of Islam
8. Al-Insaan: The Human Being
9. Speakers Bureau Guide Book
10. Islamic Perspectives
11. Islamic Understanding
12. Islam vs. Muslims
13. Health, Hygiene and Nutrition
14. Scientific Reflections from the Qur'an
15. Biological Terms in the Qur'an
16. Educational Institutions in Islam
17. Writing An Islamic Will
18. Qur'an Commentary in Summary
19. Book of Pledges
20. Selected Verses From Qur'an
21. Visit and Reflect

These and other books will not be published unless someone like you comes forward and extends a hand of help. You may sponsor any of the above books, or any number of copies of a particular book.

Your help in any capacity is greatly needed even to pay the previous debts to the printers.

The foundation is tax-exempt from the IRS and your donations are tax-deductible. The Employer Identification Number with the I.R.S. is **36-377-4566.**

For more information, or to send your donation, please contact:
Foundation for Islamic Knowledge

P.O. Box 665
Lombard, IL 60148 USA
Phone: (630) 495-4817 / Fax: (630) 627-8894

e-mail: drahmadsakr@hotmail.com website: www.ahmadsakr.com

California Address

P. O. Box 2205
Walnut, CA 91789 USA
Phone: 909-595-7800
Fax: 909-595-6391

Books Available From the Foundation for Islamic Knowledge

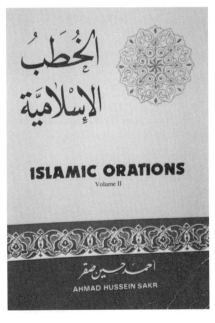

Books Available From the
Foundation for Islamic Knowledge

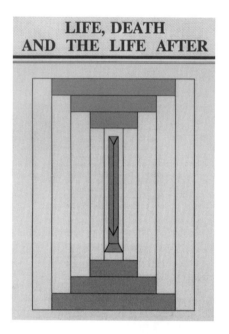

LIFE, DEATH
AND THE LIFE AFTER

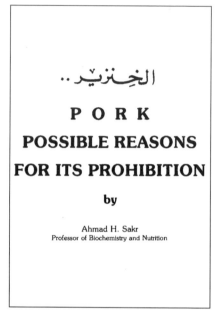

الخِنزِير ..

P O R K
POSSIBLE REASONS
FOR ITS PROHIBITION

by

Ahmad H. Sakr
Professor of Biochemistry and Nutrition

MATRIMONIAL
EDUCATION IN ISLAM

And among His Signs
Is this, that He created
For you mates from among
Yourselves, that ye may
Dwell in tranquility with them,
And He has put love
And mercy between your (hearts):
Verily in that are Signs
For those who reflect.
Qur'an (30:21)

Ahmad H. Sakr, Ph.D.

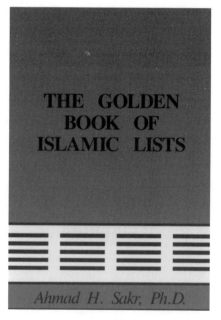

THE GOLDEN
BOOK OF
ISLAMIC LISTS

Ahmad H. Sakr, Ph.D.

Books Available From the Foundation for Islamic Knowledge

Farewell Khutbah of The Prophet ﷺ

Its Universal Values

A Muslim Guide to Food Ingredients

AHMAD H. SAKR, Ph.D.
Professor of Nutritional Biochemistry

Books Available From the
Foundation for Islamic Knowledge

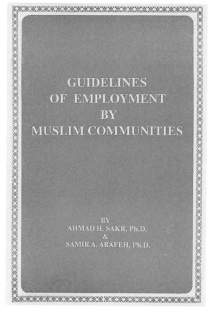

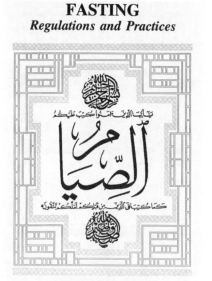

244

Books Available From the
Foundation for Islamic Knowledge

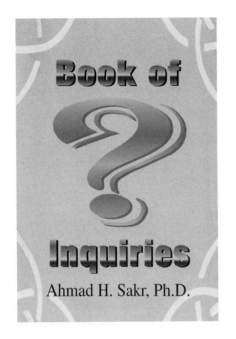

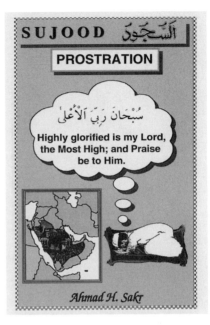

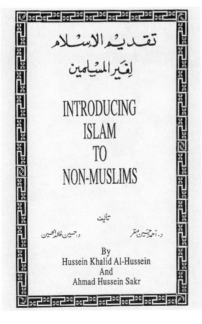

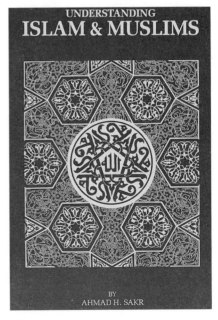

Books Available From the
Foundation for Islamic Knowledge

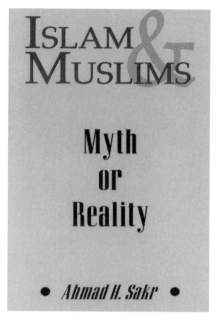

Books Available From the
Foundation for Islamic Knowledge

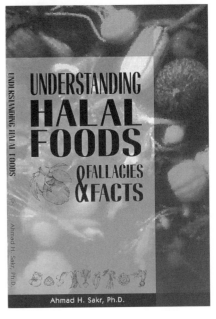

Books Available From the
Foundation for Islamic Knowledge

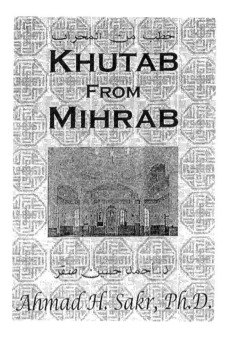

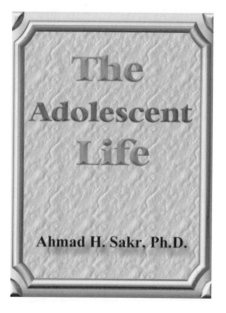

Books Available From the Foundation for Islamic Knowledge

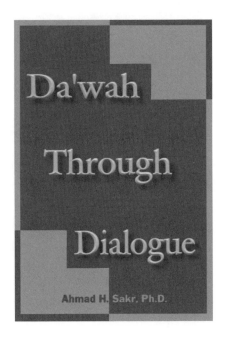

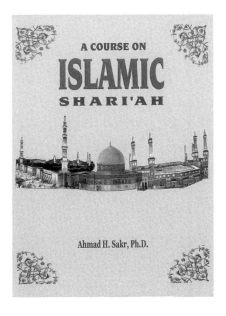

Books Available From the
Foundation for Islamic Knowledge

Books Available From the Foundation for Islamic Knowledge

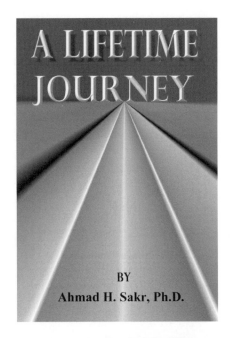

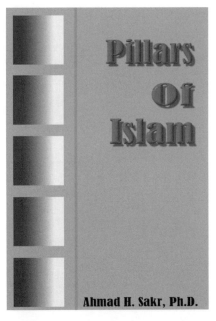

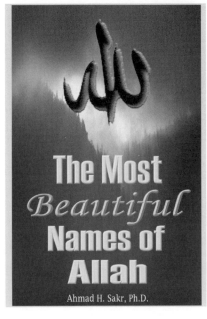

Books Available From the Foundation for Islamic Knowledge

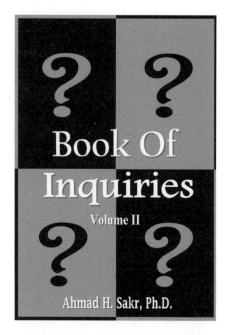

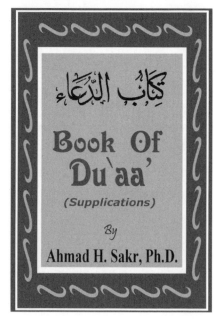

Books Available From the Foundation for Islamic Knowledge